Colorado's Great Gardens

PLAINS, MOUNTAINS & PLATEAUS

Photography by Rob Proctor

Text by Georgia Garnsey

WESTCLIFFE PUBLISHERS

Englewood, Colorado

ISBN: 1-56579-284-X

Text copyright 1998 by Georgia Garnsey. All rights reserved.
Photographs and additional text copyright 1998 by Rob Proctor. All rights reserved.
Additional photography copyright 1998 by Woody Garnsey. All rights reserved.
    pp. 10, 70, 71, 72, 73, 80, 81, 106, 107, 112, 113, 118, 119, 132, 133, 134,
    135, 136, 137, 138, 141, 142, 153.

Designers: Mark Mulvany and Tim George
Map Designer: John Wagner
Production Manager: Harlene Finn
Editor: Jennie Shortridge
Original artwork by: Rob Proctor, pp. 18, 21, 22, 28, 39, 40, 42, 44, 47, 48, 53,
    54, 64, 66, 75, 80, 83, 86, 88, 102, 104, 111, 114, 121, 124.
Published by: Westcliffe Publishers, Inc.
        P.O. Box 1261
        Englewood, Colorado 80150
Printed in: Hong Kong through Palace Press International

Library of Congress Cataloging-in-Publication Data

Proctor, Rob.
    Colorado's great gardens : plains, mountains, and plateaus /
  photography by Rob Proctor ; text by Georgia Garnsey.
      p. cm.
    ISBN 1-56579-284-X
    1. Gardens—Colorado. 2. Gardens—Colorado—Pictorial works.
  3. Gardening—Colorado. 4. Gardeners—Colorado. I. Garnsey,
  Georgia, 1947– . II. Title.
  SB466.U65C66 1998
  712'.09788—dc21

                            98-15965
                            CIP

*For more information about other fine books and calendars from Westcliffe Publishers,
please call your local bookstore, contact us at 1-800-523-3692, or write for our free
color catalog.*

First frontispiece: BUENA VISTA
Second frontispiece: STEAMBOAT SPRINGS
Opposite: GLENWOOD SPRINGS
Page 8:   GOLDEN
Page 10:   BRECKENRIDGE

Acknowledgments

Thanks to all those who helped in countless ways to produce this book of great
Colorado gardens. From moral support, to editing and technical assistance, to
providing leads, to showing us around and pointing us in the right direction, I
can't thank all of you enough:

Megan Kemper, Mariner Kemper, Hilary Jill Garnsey, Ben Peery, Jane O'Donnell,
Gaylynn Long, Ann Barrett, Judy Sellers, Greg Heartman, Panayoti Kelaidis,
Andrew Pierce, Don Eversoll, Don Williams, Buff Moore, Darlene Cornett,
Mary Stewart, Gail Donaldson, Charlotte Vowell, Ruthie Brown, Vicky Ford,
Ann Halverson, Ginny Boschen, Harold Sasaki, Mona Askwig, Susan Eubank,
Jerry Nelson, Alan Bradshaw, Carolyn Crawford, Helen Driver Flanders,
Vicky Cowart, Cynthia Cronan.

My heartfelt gratitude to all the Colorado gardeners who shared their gardens
and stories during the course of writing this book. Whether we were able to
feature a particular garden or not, all the gardens we visited were great
Colorado gardens.

Special thanks to Linda Doyle, Harlene Finn, and Kiki Sayre at Westcliffe
Publishers, and many kudos to editor Jennie Shortridge.

Most of all, thank you to Woody, for photography, for love and support, and for
making my heart bloom.

                                      —GEORGIA GARNSEY

Colorado's Great Gardens

PLATEAU GARDENS

Pages 118–143

MOUNTAIN GARDENS

Pages 62–117

PLAINS GARDENS

Pages 12–61

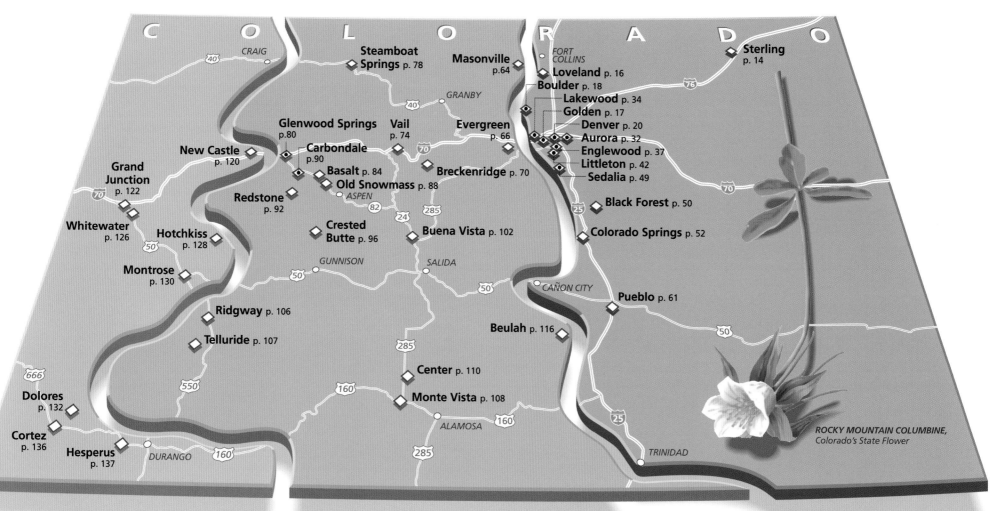

C O L O R A D O

CRAIG

Steamboat Springs p. 78

Masonville p.64

FORT COLLINS

Sterling p. 14

Loveland p. 16

Boulder p. 18

GRANBY

Lakewood p. 34

Golden p. 17

Glenwood Springs p.80

Vail p. 74

Evergreen p. 66

Denver p. 20

Aurora p. 32

New Castle p. 120

Carbondale p.90

Englewood p. 37

Littleton p. 42

Grand Junction p. 122

Basalt p. 84

Old Snowmass p. 88

Breckenridge p. 70

Sedalia p. 49

Redstone p. 92

ASPEN

Black Forest p. 50

Whitewater p. 126

Hotchkiss p. 128

Crested Butte p. 96

Buena Vista p. 102

Colorado Springs p. 52

Montrose p. 130

GUNNISON

SALIDA

CAÑON CITY

Pueblo p. 61

Ridgway p. 106

Beulah p. 116

Telluride p. 107

Dolores p. 132

Center p. 110

Cortez p. 136

Monte Vista p. 108

Hesperus p. 137

DURANGO

ALAMOSA

TRINIDAD

ROCKY MOUNTAIN COLUMBINE,
Colorado's State Flower

The Gardens

Plains

Sterling Inez Busig, Annette Smith,
    and Roberta Bryden ... 14
Loveland Cricket Coleman ... 16
Golden Mary Ellen Keskimaki ... 17
Boulder Christina Kertesz ... 18
Denver ... 20
    Susan Yetter
    Rob Proctor and David Macke
    Norma Hazen
    Hanayo Kataoka and Lily Weda
    Tom Peace
Aurora Marcia Tatroe ... 32
Lakewood ... 34
    Eileen and Patrick Mangan
    Gordon Koon
Englewood ... 37
    Donna DeSimone and
        Steven Brenman
    Anne Weckbaugh
    Linda Heller
Littleton ... 42
    Mary Ellen Tonsing
    Reed Johnson
    Mike and Carrie McLaughlin
    Marilyn Raff
    Tina Jones
Sedalia Angela Overy ... 49
Black Forest Forest Edge Gardens ... 50
Colorado Springs ... 52
    Joan Donner
    Judy Wills
    High Valley Farm
    Prudence and Beno Walker
Pueblo Karen and Bill Adams ... 61

Mountains

Masonville Lauren Springer ... 64
Evergreen ... 66
    Joan Reynolds
    Gary Sohrweid
Breckenridge ... 70
    Dodie Bingham
    Jane and Bob Hendrix
    Jane Hendrix
Vail Barbara DeVoe ... 74
Steamboat Springs ... 78
    Barbara Walker and Chip Shevlin
    Kendall and Chapman Geer
Glenwood Springs ... 80
    Vi Lake and Stormy Werking
    Naomi and Ed Neimann
Basalt ... 84
    Lynn Nichols
    Angela Foster
Old Snowmass Laurie McBride ... 88
Carbondale Katherine Ware ... 90
Redstone ... 92
    Peter and Ann Martin
    Clark and Bonnie Cretti
Crested Butte ... 96
    Marnie Easley and
        Woody Sherwood
    Rosie Catmur
    Maura Bailey
    Nancy Serfass
    Char Hansen
    Susan Lohr
Buena Vista ... 102
    Barbara Pasic
    Jim Ludwig
    Jamie Barron

Ridgway Lyle Braund ... 106
Telluride Rich Salem ... 107
Monte Vista Gloria Rios ... 108
Center ... 110
    Karen Perrin
    Dorothy Martin
Beulah ... 116
    Pat Flynn
    Samm Carter

Plateaus

New Castle Rosie and Cleyo Ferrin ... 120
Grand Junction ... 122
    Arlen and Virginia Beemer
    Tony and Allison Richards
Whitewater Susan and Gene Alexander ... 126
Hotchkiss Adam Silverstein
        and Valerie Stone ... 128
Montrose Fred Maxted ... 130
Dolores ... 132
    Four Seasons Nursery
    Karen Holmgren
Cortez Tammy and Steve Haley ... 136
Hesperus ... 137
    Suzy McCleary
    Blue Lake Ranch
    Linda and Trent Taylor

# Preface

It was nearly midnight. I drove on I-25 between Walsenburg and Pueblo, the shimmering black pavement recently washed by a passing rain shower. The storm had moved on, a riveting show of lightning illuminating the plains to the east. The musty sweet smell of sagebrush enveloped my truck and flowed through the panel vents. A week's worth of freshly shot Velvia film was safely tucked in the camera bag sitting beside me as I headed home. It was the end of June.

I thought about those photos. I hoped I hadn't screwed them up. I thought about the awesome grandeur of this state (even though my brain never actually landed on the words "awesome grandeur") and the lovely gardens and their charming owners. I also felt slightly overwhelmed, knowing that I still had at least fifty more gardens to shoot. "What in the world am I doing?" I asked aloud.

I'm not a good traveler: I sleep poorly in motels, forget to pack shaving cream or socks, and my back gets sore on long trips. I'd much rather be at home working in my own garden. That's what I'm good at and that's where I should stay. But when the opportunity to photograph the great gardens of Colorado came up, I couldn't say no, despite my reservations (or, as it turned out, the lack of them when I tried to find a vacant room in many a mountain town full of tourists).

Being a gardener as well as a photographer made this project special. I know exactly what it takes to create a garden. I understand what makes a gardener tick. Though the people whose gardens are shown in this book are vastly different in many ways—in age, in occupation, in ethnic background, and in a hundred other ways—they all share one trait: modesty. I didn't meet a single gardener during the course of this project who didn't offer some sort of apology about his or her garden. Though most were justifiably proud of the beds they tend, some expressed a shy side when it came to their gardens. "See what you think," they'd say. "You don't have to use if it you don't want to—it's kind of a weedy mess right now."

They were wrong. I'd unload compliments as quickly as camera equipment. Many would accept them, but hastily point out that the slugs had made coleslaw out of their hostas or that elk had ruined the lilies or that winds had blown the delphiniums to the ground the night before. I've seen a few perfect gardens in my day—although I've never come close myself—but perfection isn't what this book's about. It's about the love of plants and the people who grow them. Even though the gardeners faces aren't shown here (I said they were shy: "You can shoot the garden but for heaven's sake don't show me!"), in many ways the photographs reveal the portraits of the people who tend them.

On rare occasion, the modest words at the other end of the telephone line proved to be true. The garden was a weedy mess, and no amount of photographic trickery could make a silk purse out of a sow's ear. Chalk it up to experience. On the other hand, I didn't get to every great garden in the state. Hail pounded some of the best, sometimes just a heartbreaking day before I was scheduled to shoot them. In other cases, I simply ran out of time. Sometimes I just couldn't figure out how to be in two places at once. Too many gardens seemed to peak at the exact same moment, usually a thousand miles apart. It's a risky business, we all soon realized, to attempt to shoot eighty gardens in a single season.

Just getting to a garden didn't mean that I'd complete the shoot. Colorado's brilliant sunshine makes these glorious gardens possible, but it's the photographer's enemy. I like to shoot in early morning light (even if my eyes have trouble focusing at that hour, especially after an evening of tossing and turning in a motel), but I really prefer a cloudy day. We don't get that very often here, at least not the dreamily romantic clouds that are the hallmark of English garden photography. Sometimes I'd wait around all day, reading in my truck, in order to have ten minutes to shoot. I read some great novels during those times.

I remember waiting for a cloud—any cloud—to float over Mary Ellen Tonsing's garden in Littleton. We sat and drank iced tea under her gazebo on that hot July day, lamenting that our gardens were suffering from the lack of rain (though it seemed to me that her garden looked pretty darned good; even if she was feeling the stress, the garden didn't show it.) At about four o'clock, a single cloud settled overhead. My tripod was already in position to get what I considered the key shot—the gazebo floating like a luxury liner in a sea of flowers. "You have to get this right," I reminded myself. That cloud was the only one that day, but I got my shot. In the imperfect worlds of gardening and photography, it sometimes comes as a great relief when a near-perfect moment happens.

When clouds boil up in the Colorado sky, as they often do on summer afternoons, it usually means that strong winds and thunderstorms are on the way. That also means that there's very little time to shoot. The session at the Coleman garden near Loveland could have been my last. I got there just as the sky began to blacken, but the light from across the lake was mesmerizing. I rushed to compose a shot as the rain began. Thunder boomed across the lake and white-hot flashes of lightning struck uncomfortably close to where I stood with my metal tripod and camera. I hurriedly fumbled with the shot, thinking that I might as well have the steel shaft of a golf club held above my head.

Not all of the shoots held such drama. Most were relatively easy, made even more so by the subjects. Most shots take care and concentration, but the gardens portrayed in this book are so lovely that a grade-school boy with his first camera could have done a decent job. I don't mean to sound nonchalant. When I'm shooting, and the light is right and the wind is calm, I get excited. I start to sweat and I breathe rapidly. I sprint around the garden hoping to capture it all before the magic moment fades.

There was such a magic moment in the San Luis Valley in September. It had been a lousy couple of days. I wanted more shots at Karen Perrin's and Gloria and Dan Rios' gardens. The wind wouldn't stop and I couldn't buy a cloud. With the sun setting, I drove along the highway, disappointed, thinking I'd need to spend at least another day trying to get the shots. I screeched to a halt at the sight of a fence covered with what looked like a million sweet peas— this garden wasn't on my list, but what an opportunity. I took a chance, hastily introduced myself to Dorothy Martin, and begged to take photos of her garden. My camera blinked ominously at me, indicating a low battery. The sky turned from pink to lavender as the light failed. I cursed under my breath as I came to the end of the roll and reloaded as fast as possible. Darkness fell. I wondered if I'd captured what I'd seen.

Several days later, I got my film back from the lab. The Perrin shots—fine, Rios—good, Martin—yes! The photo gods had been with me. I love that shot of sweet peas. I love the lady who planted those sweet peas. I love living and gardening in this wonderful state. I'm lucky I got to do this job.

But I still hate motels.

—*Rob Proctor*

Introduction

My love of gardening has deep roots. I'm not a botanist; in fact, I struggle to remember the correct botanical names for plants. While I love growing things, I'm one of those gardeners who runs to the nursery and succumbs to the plants I like best—frothy, ruffled plants in pastel colors that may thrive in my garden borders and may not.

My parents were addicted to gardening. I watched them plant gardens from Michigan to Missouri to California to Connecticut. In every location, my father grew orchids and my mother grew roses. I was the one weeding in the background, swearing I would never have a garden, no matter where I lived. But somehow the gardening addiction took hold and grew.

I had lived in Colorado for fifteen years when my mother died. When I went to Florida to take care of final arrangements and close up her home, a row of coral 'Tropicana' roses in her front border cried out to me. "Take us home," they said. And I did. Those tender roses survived a five-hour plane ride placed at my feet as carry-ons, and weeks in my refrigerator back home in Denver. They even took to my backyard weed patch when I planted them during a May blizzard. The next year, they flowered in extravagant, bright coral blooms. My mind reeled. The successful transplanting from a lush, tropical climate to the harsh conditions of the plains seemed improbable, even miraculous, to me. As the roses flourished, I decided my mother was trying to tell me something—perhaps to get serious about Colorado gardening.

I read everything I could about the unique and surprising growing conditions of my region. I learned that roses growing in the dry and sunny Colorado climate were free of the diseases and pests fostered by moister conditions. In fact, the only setback my 'Tropicana' roses experienced in Colorado was when my two dogs ate them—blooms, thorns, and rootstock—to the ground.

Next I studied about the variety of native and drought-tolerant plants that thrive in Colorado, and the techniques—like creating microclimates, amending soil, and mulching—that allow a wide variety of plants to grow despite harsh growing conditions. Through my travels across the state, I saw the surprising variety of gardens that flourish in Colorado's distinct regions. I marveled at gardens inspired by the mountain meadows, windswept plateaus, or wide open plains around them.

It was in my own backyard that the idea of a book about Colorado gardens emerged. One summer day, my neighbor Gaylynn Long leaned across the wrought iron fence that separated our gardens and suggested the project. She would help with research and I would do the writing. As the former gardening editor for *Colorado Homes & Lifestyles* (my first article was entitled "Rites of Roses: Dry, sunny conditions prove no thorn in the side of Denver rosarians"), I brought initial contacts and experience to the effort. After much brainstorming, we decided on our concept. We would write a book that described the diversity of Colorado's gardens from the plains, mountain, and plateau regions. We would portray the surprises, challenges, and blessings of gardening in Colorado. And we would tell the stories behind these gardens and their gardeners.

After finding Westcliffe, a publisher as intrigued as we were with the idea, and Rob Proctor, a talented photographer willing to undertake a summer's worth of photographing gardens across the state, Gaylynn and I got to work. We called garden clubs, plant nurseries, chambers of commerce, and landscape architects in search of great gardens to feature. Our criteria were simple. We looked for gardens that reflected their regional landscape, gardens that people described with a catch in their throat, and most of all, gardens that evolved through the efforts, knowledge, imagination, and love of down-to-earth gardeners. We didn't include gardens installed by experts. However, a few gardens that evolved through a collaboration between gardeners and landscape architects passed our "real gardeners' gardens" test.

Then the true adventure began. Rob, Gaylynn, and I each conducted our own cross-state gardening treks. My husband Woody joined me as navigator, back-up photographer, and truest and dearest of friends on my trips. While tracking down gardens, interviews, and photographs, we accumulated enough war stories to fill volumes. Gaylynn was caught in a fierce lightning storm as she drove across the eastern plains; Rob walked into a very clean plate glass window instead of into the garden behind it in Steamboat Springs; Woody and I were chased by a Doberman pinscher guarding his owner's garden in the San Luis Valley. Woody stared the dog down as I tried in vain to scramble up a smooth adobe wall.

And then there was the joy of it. On our tour across the state, Woody and I experienced Colorado in the full sweep of its beauty. Gardeners in every city and town welcomed us, and with generosity and warmth they shared plants, seeds, and insights about their gardens and their communities. We received tips about where to hike, where to see wildflowers, and where to find more great gardens. Our only regrets were not having the time to track down all the gardens and reaching some after their blooming peaks.

The gardens we visited reflected the diverse ecological regions of the state. There were gardens featuring native junipers, sage, and cacti; gardens of larkspur and columbines and penstemons; gardens of Asiatic lilies, roses, and hollyhocks. We met gardeners who inspired us with their design sense, their imagination, and their fortitude in the face of seemingly impossible growing conditions. We heard at least fifty different solutions for deterring deer. We learned ingenious ways to amend soil, whether sandy, clay, or near-cement. We saw gardens of such beauty that the vision will stay with us forever.

Colorado's Great Gardens: Plains, Mountains & Plateaus is the result of this collaborative effort. Colorado's different regions are packed with great gardens, and we were able to capture only some of them. Hopefully, this work provides an intriguing glimpse of the range and scope of the state's gardens.

In writing this book, I have tried to let each gardener tell his or her own story. The text is sprinkled with as many direct quotes as possible, and regional gardening facts and tips are woven throughout. Because I found touring Colorado's gardens a great way to experience the state, I included area descriptions and historical data in some garden stories. Most of all, I hope that I've captured the talent and passion of the featured gardeners and the magic of the gardens they create.

—GEORGIA GARNSEY

Colorado Plains

"It gave me a strange sensation to embark upon the Plains. Plains, plains everywhere, plains generally level, but elsewhere rolling in long undulations, like the waves of a sea which had fallen asleep. They are covered thinly with buff grass, the withered stalks of flowers, Spanish bayonet, and a small beehive-shaped cactus. One could gallop all over them" (Isabella L. Bird, *A Lady's Life in the Rocky Mountains*).

Traveling through Fort Collins in 1873, English adventuress Isabella Bird described the golden, sunny expanse of the eastern two-thirds of Colorado. Early settlers of the plains, many from New England, experienced the same sense of wonder as they began living in the vast, treeless region. In their first gardens, they attempted to recreate the gardens of moisture-loving plants they remembered from back home. The plains quickly withered these first gardening ventures. In later years, horticultural pioneers like George Kelly, who wrote *Rocky Mountain Horticulture Is Different* in 1951, introduced gardening techniques and outlooks that fit the unique growing conditions of the region. Several gardeners in this section frequented the plant nursery Kelly owned from the 1940s through the 1960s, where native, drought-tolerant plants were sold.

Ornamental grasses were among Kelly's suggestions for native plants to add character, definition, and interest to Colorado gardens. Gardens included in the plains section feature a variety of grasses. In the northeastern town of Sterling, a mother and her two daughters rave about the way grasses catch light, move in the wind, and add warm color and striking dimension to their gardens. Stately pampas and Karl Foerster grasses, arching fountain grass, and lower tufts of blue fescue and blue oat grasses mix with veronicas, campanulas, penstemons, and delphiniums in their garden borders.

Along with plentiful sunshine, the plains region has low rainfall, severe winters, alkaline soil, and freak storms. Amending soil with peat, manure, and compost is the first priority of plains gardeners, while water conservation is their top concern. Native plants that naturally withstand the area's tough conditions and bring the beauty of the region into domestic spaces appear in gardens from Sterling south to Pueblo. Plants native to regions with similar climates, like South Africa and the steppe countries of Asia, are increasingly popular. Panayoti Kelaidis, curator of the Rock Alpine Garden at Denver Botanic Gardens, introduced many plants from other countries that thrive in area gardens. His influence has spread throughout the Rocky Mountain region.

The rich diversity of native and introduced plants available to plains gardeners is matched only by the many ways these plants are integrated into garden landscapes. In Boulder, clipped shrubs of gray-green germander and santolina form patterns around herbs and roses. Although an English tradition, this informal version of an herb knot garden looks at home against the backdrop of a mesa and cottonwood trees. On a windy slope in Golden, Asiatic lilies and Canadian roses grow with irises, Russian sage, and Rocky Mountain penstemons in a colorful blending of hybrid, native, and drought-tolerant perennials and bulbs. A Japanese garden in Denver is a striking mixture of eastern and western influences and plant materials. Ponderosa pines sculpted into windswept forms line a pond blooming with water lilies, while a

DENVER

stone Buddha sits among peonies, hens and chicks, and Johnny jump-ups at the top of a rounded berm. Spreading under euonymus, yew, and Siberian pea shrubs in a Colorado Springs garden are sage, Apache plumes, and Scotch brooms. A Pueblo landscaper has installed zebra, ruby, and pampas grasses around the lions' cages at the city's zoo. In her gardens at home, plants that grow in the plains around Pueblo—penstemons, Blackfoot daisies, prairie Indian paintbrush, and Rocky Mountain zinnias— flow over a berm with ice plants and gazanias from South Africa.

All-season interest is another quality of gardens on the plains, where every season is distinct. Forests of trees—spruces, pines, firs, maples, oaks, and lindens—bring green hues and occasional flowers to Denver gardens in spring and summer, splashes of fiery color in the fall, and the stark beauty of their leafless branches during winter months. Since cottonwoods and chokecherries are the only trees that greeted early visitors to the area, the range of trees lining Denver's streets and filling its yards attests to the longing and vision of the city's first residents.

Galloping over the plains today, Isabella Bird might be surprised.

BLACK FOREST

ENGLEWOOD

Sterling

Inez Busig and her daughters, Annette Smith and Roberta Bryden, like their gardens to swing and sway. Residents of Sterling, located in the northeastern corner of Colorado, this family of gardeners has inherited an appreciation for the grasses native to their region. The Pawnee National Grasslands are located thirty miles west of town, and serve as inspiration for the women's garden compositions.

Having lived most of their lives on the family cattle ranch outside of town, the three now live and garden close to each other in town. They all praise the virtues of the tall grasses that move gracefully in the seasonal winds that blow from the high plains of Wyoming through their gardens.

"To me," says Roberta, "a garden is not just a splash of color—it's got to have motion and movement." She uses grasses and old farm machinery as focal points in the perennial beds that curve through her backyard. She placed the family ranch grinding wheel in the center of the main flower bed, and boards from the old corral fence line the garden path. The path deliberately leads behind the masses of colorful flowers because, as Roberta says, "There's not a garden on earth that's one-sided."

Pampas and Karl Foerster grasses are two of Roberta's favorite ornamentals. Their slender blades and wispy plumes add texture and soft color as a backdrop for veronicas, Shasta daisies, daylilies, and bee balms swirling through the summer garden. In the fall, dried plumes complement the rich colors of asters, chrysanthemums, marigolds, and cannas.

Around the corner and down the street is Annette's "kid-friendly" garden, where there's just enough lawn for the kids to play games. Annette's three daughters love playing in the landscape where they're free to pick bouquets of flowers and take imaginary trips on walkways that ramble through trees, shrubs, and flower beds in the yard.

Annette favors ornamental grasses because they're hardy, low maintenance, and "give a show in every season." She mixes the gracefully arching

fountain grass and luxuriant pampas grass with lower tufts of blue fescue and blue oat grasses. During summer, a variety of flowers and vegetables wander among the vertical foliage. The orange-reds of pumpkins, gourds, and rose hips glow against the mix of tawny, silvery grasses in the fall.

On the south side of the house, Annette and her husband designed a large rock garden using boulders collected from Pawnee Pass, a sandstone formation outside of town. In the spring, the garden bursts into color with masses of shell pink soapwort and blue veronica.

After forty years of gardening on the family ranch, Inez now enjoys helping in her daughters' in-town gardens. It is her own creation, however, that is the real tribute to her passion and gardening skills. Residents of her new condominium complex call it "Miss Inez's Botanic Garden," referring to the seventy-five-foot-long berm in the complex packed with annuals, perennials, and grasses. Condominium residents pitched in with donations of soil to create the berm. The garden was started with transplants of phlox, chrysanthemums, irises, and globe thistles from her ranch gardens, and Inez later added flax, asters, columbines, delphiniums, and petunias. Her daughters finally inspired her to mix ornamental grasses with the perennials and annuals.

"I wasn't very impressed with the idea of ornamental grasses at first, because in the country the wild grasses were so invasive. But I liked the billowing plumes of pampas grass in Roberta and Annette's yards and decided to give them a try," Inez says. "Now the pampas grass gives character to my garden. I like to leave the tops on their stalks in winter because they show which way the wind is blowing."

Sharing gardening insights and perspectives has provided fertile ground for Inez and her daughters' gardens.

Loveland

Cricket Coleman gazes past the floral waves of white peonies before her to a life-sized bronze sculpture of the Lady of the Lake, silhouetted against the blue expanse of Boyd Lake. The glistening white blossoms echo the white-capped peaks of the Mummy Range and Longs Peak in the distance, while the statue by the lake, inspired by Cricket's love of Arthurian legend, completes the sense of an idyllic, far-off world.

Cricket lives in Loveland, located between the northeastern plains and the Colorado Rockies, with Rocky Mountain National Park to the west. Loveland's bronze foundries and public art programs make it a haven for sculptors as well as a nationally-known Valentine remailing center. The city's spectacular natural surroundings provide a wonderful backdrop for the area's many gardeners. Every summer, the Junior League of Loveland sponsors a tour that showcases the best gardens.

"I attended my first garden tour in 1992, when my garden was a patch of weeds and scraggly shrubs and trees," says Cricket. "The gardens I saw inspired me, and I decided that someday I would be part of a garden tour, too."

After years of amending her soil, building flagstone-lined borders and pathways, and landscaping with perennials, shrubs, and trees, Cricket's dream came true. In l996, her lush gardens were featured in both the Junior League Garden Tour and the Tri-State Garden Contest. Cricket received first place in the flower garden category at the Tri-State event.

Winding past herb gardens and circular flower beds brimming with peonies, phlox, daylilies, and lady's mantle, a boardwalk leads to the statue and the lake. A stone wall draped with climbing roses and trumpet vines borders the walk and stretches the length of the yard. Encircling a flagstone patio at the end of the yard is a border of hot-colored perennials —fiery red daylilies, yellow coreopsis, and brilliant blue salvias.

Describing her garden philosophy, Cricket says, "My garden is where I can express myself with abandon." Whimsical and free-spirited, Cricket's garden has fast become a legend on the eastern plains.

Mary Ellen Keskimaki

Golden

One summer day as she trimmed shrubs in her front yard, Mary Ellen Keskimaki felt a curious tingle down her spine. Turning around, she saw eight green racer snakes eyeing her as they lay coiled on the pathway, enjoying the afternoon sun. "What sweethearts," says Mary Ellen. "They looked like lots of little Dino the Dinosaurs, swarming all around me, so friendly and unafraid. Now they patrol the garden. They really cut down on slugs."

This may not be the usual reaction to three-foot-long reptiles, but Mary Ellen enjoys the solitary immersion in nature that many other Colorado gardeners describe. "I love the activity in my garden—like the sound of insects humming away among the plants," she says. "Besides the racer snakes, there's a bull snake who suns in a patch of mint to the side of the house. I choose plants that attract living things, like hummingbirds, butterflies, and birds."

Mary Ellen lives on a windy hillside overlooking the flat top of North Table Mountain in Golden, due west of Denver. She brought truckloads of topsoil, peat moss, and manure into her yard to amend her rocky clay soil. Surrounding her home are gardens well worth the preliminary effort and expense.

Across the steep slope of the front yard, bright rose-colored Asiatic lilies, deep blue irises, Russian sage, and lavenders rise above mats of hot pink ice plant, dianthus, soapwort, and purple-blue veronica. Ponderosa pines, aspens, and currant bushes weave among deeply veined rocks through the plantings. A Russian hawthorn packed with white blooms shades an area to the side of the house where forget-me-nots, campanulas, and catmints swirl in shades of blue around a stone birdbath. On the hillside behind the house, Rocky Mountain penstemons throw out purple spires in June.

Mary Ellen's Hungarian hunting dog, Duke, enjoys the garden, too. The dark crimson blossoms of the floribunda rose 'Europeana' mass around the entrance to Duke's dog house. Along a nearby fence, the huge pale blue flowers of 'Ramona' clematis wind among the coral pink blossoms of 'Gold Flame' honeysuckle.

Mary Ellen suggests amending soil in January and mulching with pine needles for a Colorado garden that will please humans and animals alike—and even snakes.

Boulder

"I love working outdoors, and I love raising plants from seed. In our hectic, often artificial world it helps me stay grounded," says Christina Kertesz, a thoroughly grounded Boulderite who was born in Finland of Swedish parents.

Christina's gardening passion has engaged her entire family in transforming the acre surrounding their home into beautiful gardens. Against the backdrop of Davidson Mesa, her husband Peter drags in topsoil for raised beds and rocks for retaining walls. Her sons build the walls and lay the flagstone steps that lead through gardens bordered by cottonwood trees and expanses of open field. "The only thing that stops Mom's gardens are power lines," says her youngest son Chris.

Whatever the restrictions, the results are spectacular. Outside the Kertesz' kitchen, a knot garden of clipped gray-green santolina and germander shrubs encompasses miniature roses and sage, thyme, and ornamental oreganos. Lavenders and deep purple salvias skirt the area and lead down steps to a northern facing slope where an apple tree shades huge hostas and coral bells. Yellow daylilies shining among deep red shrub roses continue the parade to the wide beds of perennials, shrubs, and small trees lining the flat expanse directly behind the house.

"There are no prima donnas in my garden," says Christina as she surveys the waves of brilliant blooms and varying shades of green, gray, and silver that make up her central garden area. "These are all tough plants."

Stalwart coneflowers, yarrows, catmint, and white fireweed spread among red-leaf rose, daphne, viburnum, and buddleia shrubs in the sunny borders. Spires of white 'Album' verbascum with maroon centers rise above pink 'Ballerina' geraniums; daisies and the frothy lavender spikes of goat's rue mingle with apricot daylilies. Pink mallows growing among white roses make for another pleasing combination of plants. There are surprises, too. At one corner of the border, yellow daylilies peek through the smoky haze of a six-foot-tall bronze fennel plant. Farther on, a giant sea kale presides over red pincushion flowers growing among purple sheets of woolly veronica. Deep blue Rocky Mountain penstemons appear and reappear throughout the flower beds.

"My palette of plants consisted mainly of roses, peonies, and delphiniums until I saw a Rocky Mountain penstemon for the first time," says Christina. "I fell in love with it. The showy spires of bell-shaped flowers bring such beauty and dimension to my plantings. I let this perennial reseed all over my garden."

Christina also favors the Japanese anemones that she found in an abandoned yard. After digging them up and over-wintering them in her vegetable garden, Christina found permanent homes for them in her borders where they continue to thrive. She has identified the fall-blooming perennials as 'Honorine Jobert,' a white variety, and the pink as 'September Charm.' "Rescuing plants from an old garden and giving them a chance to grow in a new garden gives me a sense of continuity," she says. "Gardeners who don't even know each other can pass along plants from one generation to the next."

The wooden gazebo standing at the back of the yard affords different views of the garden areas. Plantings weave together in scalloped patterns of varying heights, colors, and textures. Under dwarf apricot trees, pale yellow umbrellas of meadow rues blend with the gentian blue tubular flowers of *Corydalis flexuosa* 'Blue Panda.' Apricot sprays of plume poppy arch over purple irises and mounds of chartreuse lady's mantle. Growing at the border's edge are pink and yellow primroses, reminiscent of Christina's grandmother's garden in Sweden. Clematis vines in varying hues of blue and purple spread across lattice fences, and light pink 'New Dawn' roses clamber up rebar teepees that stand between the borders. Bristlecone pines, 'Seckel' pear trees, and small oaks that Christina grew from seed skirt the garden's perimeter.

Standing among her bountiful, fragrant, and magical gardens, Christina promises Peter and Chris that she will build a fence next, and create no more flower beds. The two men exchange knowing glances, look at the beauty around them, and smile.

Denver

Susan Yetter thinks of her garden as a nautilus shell. "The garden starts with a kernel, a central core, and then it unfolds and builds from there," she says. "But it always goes back to that beginning, that first seed, that first idea and source. The garden is full of lessons on a spiritual plane."

Susan loves to sit on a high berm in the center of her garden in the morning. Coffee cup in hand, she contemplates the tidal wave of color and texture around her. Flowering perennials swirl among native shrubs and trees in a setting that is inspired by Moorish architecture, Zen Buddhist philosophy, an affinity for the southwestern United States, and a sensibility for the immediate surroundings.

Susan's garden is located in the front yard of her northwest Denver home. Roses, clematis, honeysuckle, and trumpet vines clamber over the wrought iron fence and entry archway that stand between her property and the street. Lattice work and cedar fences covered with more vining plants form parallel sides of the garden enclosure, while the Yetters' sprawling one-story home serves as the fourth boundary of the rectangular space. "It's important that the garden is in the front where people can see it," says Susan. "The fences are all friendly and inviting—like in Latin America and Spain where there are walls in front of the house, but passersby can peek over the enclosures into the inner courtyard."

Once inside the yard, a whole new world opens up. Paths lead through berms of drought-tolerant penstemons, salvias, veronicas, mallows, irises, and roses. The silver-grays of saltbush and astragalus shrubs weave through the plantings. Ornamental grasses, with their upright structure and silver and buff-colored hues, are key to Susan's garden design. "The grasses are the calm backdrop that tie everything together," she says.

Found objects are another unifying garden theme. When the viaduct underneath Denver's Union Station in lower downtown was excavated, Susan was there to collect the late-1800s-era pavers,

relics no one else wanted. She incorporated the pavers into the system of pathways winding through her garden. A porcelain hand-washing basin retrieved from the Brown Palace Hotel is now a terrarium housing a collection of succulent plants. Sandstone windowsills and cornice mouldings from a turn-of-the-century Denver elementary school rest at intervals throughout the garden, supporting pots of petunias, statues, shells, and collections of stones. Roses, veronicas, and coral bells slumber inside rusted bed frames while porcelain berry, a vigorous climber with dark green leaves, twines along a teepee of old spades, rakes, and hoes. Susan likens the intense blue of the berries to the deep hues glistening from plates of fine china.

The beams from an old grape arbor support the lattice roof of a ramada, or open porch, in a corner of the garden. Red-leaf roses blooming in thousands of star-shaped pink flowers join with the magenta blossoms of the hardy floribunda 'Nearly Wild' to form a backdrop of color and fragrance. Filling the light-dappled shelter are comfortable chairs that offer quiet resting places to appreciate the surrounding beauty.

Although every season in her garden offers new perspectives and challenges, Susan enjoys the autumn months most of all. "In the fall, the garden is soft and golden," she says. "It resembles a tapestry with subtle patterns weaving through it." As the multi-hued riot of summer blooms fade, the striking reds of amur maples and the yellows of aspen trees shelter 'Purple Dome' asters, coneflowers, Maximillian sunflowers, and the reds and purples of sumac, hawthorn, and viburnum shrubs. An informal hedge of Karl Foerster grass brings a burnished finish to the earth-toned plantings.

With its diversity of plant material and visual interest, Susan's garden occupies a modest front yard space. But what is space in a garden that simulates the intricate structure of a nautilus shell? "I try to see how everything I find can interlock into one coherent place," says Susan, a gardener, philosopher, teacher, and artist rolled into one resounding whole.

Denver

It's a charming old story: a gardener buys an aging house and patiently restores its ramshackle garden to its former glory. "For me, it's a fable," says author and plantsman Rob Proctor. "True, I bought an old house, but there was no garden to restore—and I have little patience."

Rob and his partner David Macke set to work creating the garden when they moved to northwest Denver in 1993. It was a summer of sod stripping, rototilling, laying brick patios and flagstone paths, and planting, not to mention house painting, building fences, and directing crews removing diseased elm trees. "Frankly, it was chaos," Rob says.

While designing the garden, which sits on a flat lot of nearly an acre, he tried to envision a garden that suited the late-Victorian style of the house. The answer was a framework of borders, best viewed from the roof of the folly, a free-standing architectural feature with a spiral staircase to the top. From this height, the structure of the garden becomes apparent. Straight lines and half circles serve as a picture frame, enclosing an ever-changing painting of plants. That's another old story—the gardener as artist—but in this case it's true. Rob is a botanical illustrator whose work has been exhibited at the Smithsonian Institution. "I'm always trying to find space to grow new plants I want to draw," he says.

To make a series of experiments look like a cohesive garden, he groups plants in theme borders. His favorites are the twin pastel borders that the folly overlooks. With a backdrop of brick columns and clematis-covered latticework, these borders feature pale-toned perennials. Butter yellow, lavender-blue, and pink comprise the main palette, enhanced by liberal strokes of chartreuse. Other borders showcase particular colors: one is filled with sunset colors of coral and bronze, another with mauve, maroon, and rosy purple, and yet another is devoted to yellow and blue blossoms. Rob also designed a white and silver

border. Stuffed with white-flowered perennials and gray foliage, especially that provided by myriad artemisias, the border shows to best effect—like much of the garden—at dawn and dusk. Rob credits the beauty of the billowing borders to Colorado's brilliant sunshine and low humidity. "This is heaven for a vast array of perennials," he says.

Woodland perennials flourish on the east and west sides of the house beneath mature ash, maple, spruce, apple, and crab apple trees. In a small sunken garden, the result of a chance discovery of the brick foundation of an old building, choice shade-loving plants—primulas, pulmonarias, and corydalis—find a suitable home.

At the other extreme are several areas of the garden that require minimal irrigation. This includes the exasperating area between the street and sidewalk that many western gardeners refer to as the "hell strip." This area of Rob's yard teems with native plants and adaptable exotics that thrive with little additional watering in mineral-rich, low-humus native soil.

Rob's experimentation isn't limited to his borders. The patios feature over 500 containers. "It's gotten completely out of hand," he says. "Staging and planting them takes an entire week in May." The pots contain bold tropical plants, such as palms, bananas, and cannas, as well as fragrant flowers like Oriental lilies that make dining and entertaining outdoors a special pleasure.

According to Rob, the entire garden is meant to evolve over time. "A garden is meant to change," he reflects. "I think this garden will keep me busy for the rest of my life."

Denver

A line of majestic spruce trees screens Norma Hazen's English Tudor home from view. Once inside the property, visitors are greeted by a forest of trees sheltering wide, curved beds of perennials, annuals, grasses, and shrubs that circle an expanse of lawn. Located in a residential area near one of west Denver's most congested streets, the forested oasis is a result of Norma's long-range gardening philosophy.

"My husband and I moved to this neighborhood in 1962, when there were nothing but elm trees growing everywhere," says Norma. "I noticed that one of my neighbors had planted a group of firs in their yard, and I thought how the trees were such a relief from the flatness of the plains. I decided that we would be in our house for a long time, and I'd plant trees that would be here for a long time as well."

The strategy paid off. The varying textures, shapes, and green shadings of pines, firs, maples, oaks, and lindens towering along the acre lot's perimeter bring dramatic depth to the colorful plantings beneath them. At least 100 trees, most planted from seed, make the flat yard into a breathtaking parkland setting.

Beautiful and unusual combinations of plants fill the garden's flower beds through the seasons. In spring, the blues of columbines and Jacob's ladders swirl among the heavy blossoms of bright pink peonies. Irises in shades of purple, magenta, and white roam among the silvery foliage and purple-red flowers of rose campions. Tumbling through the borders in a show of sparkling color are a variety of tulips and daffodils.

During summer months, bright colors predominate among Norma's plantings. Against the backdrop of ponderosa pines and white firs, yellow Asiatic lilies grow among spires of deep purple 'May Night' salvias and mounds of chartreuse lady's mantle along a west-facing border. Bright pink soapwort, dianthus, and purple and yellow pansies are scattered at the base of the plants.

On the south side of the yard, Austrian and Scotch pines stand behind an informal garden area. A wood-chip path winds past a picking garden jammed with Asiatic and Oriental hybrid lilies. Leaning against an oak tree, a ladder surrounded by sunflowers supports hyacinth bean vines, blooming in loose clusters of purple and white sweet pea–shaped flowers. Yarrows, lilies, and pink roses mix companionably among silvery lamb's ears, apricot dahlias, and fuzzy pink ageratums as the path continues to a small gazebo. Norma likes mixing annuals with perennial plants, and around the wood structure, cleome, nicotiana, and nasturtiums grow with blue and white campanulas, daisies, and black-eyed Susans. Behind the gazebo, honeysuckle and clematis vines sprawl across a wood fence that encloses the yard. "We call this our wine-tasting area, although we spend a lot of time here just relaxing and looking around," says Norma.

Thanks to a small greenhouse on the east side of the yard, Norma is able to extend her growing season and the types of plants she can grow. 'Snow Queen' hydrangeas, cannas, and ferns are some of the more unusual and tender varieties that grace the Hazens' yard through the summer months. Barrels filled with more greenhouse plants—ornamental grasses, lilies, and begonias—circle a maple tree shading the patio behind the house. Under the tree, the ground cover moneywort spreads in a mat of light green leaves and yellow flowers. Colorful ceramic pieces of broken dishes and tiles are embedded in the stone path leading to the patio and in pots that fill the area. The mosaic effect adds a touch of whimsy to the quiet, light-dappled spot.

The patio is a wonderful place to view the fall color in Norma's garden. The brilliant reds, oranges, and yellows of maples and oaks splash across the green expanse of firs and pines. Filling flower beds in red and deep pink hues are 'Autumn Joy' sedums, salvias, and Japanese anemones. Golden and rust-colored grasses lend a warm glow to the late-blooming show.

Norma can't pick a favorite season in her garden, and naming a favorite plant is close to torture for her. "There is a volunteer oak seedling that I noticed the other day, though," she admits. "I do look forward to seeing that new tree grow."

Denver

When Yoshio Kataoka moved to Denver with his wife Hanayo, son Glenn, and daughter Lily in 1945, he dreamed of a Japanese garden. A native of Hiroshima, Japan, Yoshio wanted to create a place of familiar beauty as well as to preserve part of his Japanese culture for his family. His dream was far from possible at first. Released from an internment camp after World War II, the Kataokas responded to Colorado Governor Ralph Carr's open invitation to Japanese-American citizens to resettle in the state. Carr was one of the only U.S. governors to acknowledge the grievous wrongs committed against Japanese-Americans during the war. Yoshio and his family's first home was in a small, skid row hotel near today's Sakura Square in lower downtown Denver. A bust of Governor Carr, donated by the Japanese-American community, now stands in the middle of the square.

The Kataokas' next move was to a home a block from Sloans Lake in west Denver. It is here that Yoshio (also known as Bob by many in the Denver community) built his garden. Although he died in 1986, Hanayo and Lily maintain the garden in honor of Yoshio and his dream.

"For the most part, the garden is about textures and shades of green," says Lily. "Color comes from flowering trees, a few perennials and annuals, and ground covers. The character pines are the most important garden feature." Ponderosa and Scotch pines, sculpted into wind-bent forms, stand among craggy rocks and along a stream and lily pond in the backyard garden. Lily commutes from her home every day during spring and summer to help her mother with a variety of gardening chores, but her main job to is prune the pines to maintain their eloquent silhouettes. "Each tree has its own character," says Lily. "You have to study a tree a long time to understand what it wants to say. Then you need to climb around in the tree to shape it and wire branches in place. I spend many hours pinching back needles to make the branches grow longer."

The garden, situated on a steeply rounded berm, is a seamless mix of western and eastern influences and plant materials. A wooden bridge arches over a stream in the center of the garden. At one end of the bridge, a stone Buddha sits on a rock covered with hens and chicks. Johnny jump-ups cluster about the Buddha, and bright masses of rock cress and creeping phlox spread across the berm to either side of the statue. The stream runs through the middle of the garden and connects to the lily pond at one end of the yard. Bronze cranes stand among lily pads in the pond that is surrounded by boulders, rocks, junipers, and peonies.

On the other side of the yard, along the berm's perimeter, stand a weeping cherry tree with arching branches of tiny pale pink blossoms, and peach trees flowering in semidouble rose-pink blooms. Flax, columbines, poppies, cacti, and sedums grow across the slope and around stones etched with Japanese characters. "The inscriptions speak of happiness and of how you feel in a garden," says Hanayo.

Iron Japanese lanterns line a gravel path that leads deeper into the garden to the top of the berm. This is a quiet and serene area where character pines and tree peonies with heavy magenta flowers lean over flat pools formed by the depressions in rocks. Among juniper bushes and huge gray boulders, cactus plants bloom in cup-shaped yellow and pink flowers. In the spring, daffodils, tulips, and crocuses tumble down the hill and fill the area.

"Every ten years the magnolia tree blooms," says Lily. "Usually a spring frost kills the buds, but when conditions permit, the huge white flowers are amazing—and worth the wait."

A greenhouse behind the garden contains Hanayo's collection of bonsai plants. Azaleas, camellias, junipers, maples, orange and pomegranate trees, pines, succulents, and cacti are only some of the exquisitely sculpted miniature plants "growing in a tray"—the literal translation of bonsai—and under the care of Hanayo's capable hands.

With so many wonders to savor, Hanayo loves the water lilies best. "The pond has not changed since my husband created it," she says. "And every Memorial Day, the water lilies bloom."

Denver

How professional gardeners, who spend most of their day in clients' gardens, have time and energy to work in their gardens at home is baffling. "I love plants," explains designer and gardening author Tom Peace. "The variety of species, the diversity of forms and textures, the spectrum of colors—it's all a constant source of entertainment."

Tom lives in south Denver and shares home gardening chores with his wife Diane, also a professional gardener. A summer evening's entertainment at the Peace household consists of rooting cuttings, returning client phone calls, picking vegetables for dinner, and watering flats of plants slated for planting in clients' gardens. The family cat stares endlessly at goldfish in a pond stuffed with water lilies, cannas, and other aquatic plants.

One of the first plants to greet visitors is a 'Peace' rose, complemented by sprays of snow daisy and adobe-pink yarrow. "We feel obliged to grow that rose, not only because of our name, but because we felt sorry for it," says Tom about the classic hybrid tea rose. The bush was one of the only flowering inhabitants of the otherwise Spartan landscape when the couple bought their home. While they don't usually recommend such demanding plants, this one survives with minimal fuss because previous owners planted it deeper than is ordinarily recommended in the moisture-retentive clay soil. Tom and Diane thought the rose looked lonesome in its home next to the driveway, so they designed a long border around it, planting a profusion of tough perennials that provide waves of flowers throughout the growing season. Favorite perennial performers in this border include 'Walker's Low' catmint, 'Herrenhausen' oregano, sea holly, and the golden-leaf form of blue mist spirea.

The Peace garden features hundreds of rare plants as well as tried-and-true performers that thrive with minimal care and irrigation. Many plants are selected for their adaptability to clay soil and low water requirements, but color and texture are important as well. A hallmark of Tom's garden design is vibrant color, complemented by audacious juxtaposition of foliage shape and pattern. He favors richly toned flowers that hold up well under the intensity of the Colorado sun. Tom incorporates a number of annuals and non-hardy tropical perennials such as cannas, flowering maples, classic zinnia, and lavatera.

Another border runs the length of the house and curves to follow the property line across the front lawn. Rather than erect a barrier of typical chain-link, the couple planted a flowering fence of sunflowers, black-eyed Susans, lamb's ear, and other low-maintenance flowers which bring pleasure on both sides. The goldfish pond is integrated into this garden near the front of the house. The garden behind the house supplies vegetables and herbs for the couple, who, despite their busy schedules, enjoy collaborating on the family dinner.

Tom claims that he probably would have taken longer to design this garden but he was scheduled to do a gardening segment on the Discovery Channel series *Home Matters* in July 1996. The producer decided it would be instructive to take the bare front yard of the Peace family's typical suburban home (which they had moved into two weeks before) and show how to create a garden from the ground up. "We nearly collapsed in the ninety-five degree heat during the shoot," Tom recalls. "But the garden has filled out well." The couple plans to extend the garden—in their spare time—to accommodate more experimental plants.

GOLDEN-LEAF BLUE MIST SPIREA, SEA HOLLY, AND WHITE CONEFLOWER ▶

Aurora

Marcia Tatroe

Front yard gardens get rave reviews in older neighborhoods. In the conservative suburbs, however, any departure from regulation bluegrass lawn is still a rare sight. On a quiet street just south of the Aurora city limits, Marcia and Randy Tatroe's garden is as jolting as a traveling circus come to town.

Not a blade of the original bluegrass lawn remains in the front yard. Randy insisted on keeping a small remnant of lawn around back for croquet and the family spaniel. The rest of the property, front and back, is dominated by flowers of every imaginable description. Marcia explains that they have tried dozens of trees and shrubs over the years, but most of the trees have since died. "Look around," she quips. "Trees don't grow in this part of Colorado. You can't outsmart Mother Nature." So the couple grows flowers by default.

When the Tatroe family moved into their home ten years ago, they started stripping sod even before their boxes were unpacked. They had chosen this house because two sides of the lot backed onto open space and because there wasn't much existing landscape to take out. It soon became apparent that they should have paid more attention to the soil. Newly transplanted to Colorado, the Tatroes had no idea clay could be this bad. Marcia proudly displays a chunk of the stuff on her desk as a paperweight and as a reminder of how much backbreaking work they have accomplished over the years. Soil improvement became a long-term family project. With the help of sons Kevin and Keith, everyone started digging a network of borders throughout the quarter-acre lot. Neighbors watched in astonishment as family members and truckloads of manure disappeared into deep holes on weekday evenings and weekends.

Marcia, the gardener of the household, started out with two basic goals. She wanted a verdant, full garden like the one she had left behind in England, and she wanted to use as little water as possible to do this. She remembers that Randy was highly skeptical at the time. Looking back, she says, he was right. "We've long since stopped emulating English gardens and have come to appreciate Colorado's own style," she notes. The couple embraced xeriscaping and have created a lush garden that requires a fraction of the water consumption of a typical household.

Ten years ago the Tatroes' first concern was privacy. Marcia recalls, "There wasn't any. When we came to view the house, we could clearly see the former owners sitting on their back patio from a block away." New construction cut off a view of the entire Front Range in exchange for an unobstructed panorama of neighbors' kitchens and family rooms. The Tatroes hit the fall nursery sales and started planting a screen of trees and shrubs before winter set in.

That first winter, Marcia drew a set of plans for the garden. Lack of privacy wasn't the only problem. The backyard faced southwest so the patio was scorching hot and unusable during the summer months. A large section of the hillside slumped away into open space. The perimeter fence was an abomination of chain-link fencing and rotting wood posts. The construction phase began in earnest in early spring.

When the dust finally cleared, the property was transformed. A massive wooden arbor now shades the patio and gives support to grapes and other vines. A basket-weave pattern of brick pavers conceals the old concrete slab and extends onto a second level to provide more room for entertaining. The unsightly chain-link, which was required by neighborhood covenants, is camouflaged by a new split-rail fence. The old fence timbers have been resurrected as compost bins and raised beds. Broken concrete chunks form retaining walls that hold the hill from further erosion. Berms made from piles of sod and studded with rocks create a series of rock gardens.

"This is as far as my initial vision went," admits Marcia. The rest of the garden evolved without a plan. Keith wanted a goldfish pond and was willing to do the digging, so one summer a pond appeared. A waterfall only seemed a natural accompaniment, so that went in, too. Another summer, on a whim, Randy ordered two tons of flagstone to lay over the front lawn. "That certainly caused a stir in the neighborhood," Marcia remembers. The resulting flagstone terrace now supports a tumble of ground covers, wildflowers, and rock garden plants. Mixed borders surround the flagstone and now something is always in bloom in the front yard between March and November.

Other gardens wrap around the rest of the house. That awkward rectangle between the driveway and the property line typical of suburban lots became the perfect place for xeriscaping. Native shrubs and wildflowers fill the area as well as imports from other parts of the world with climates similar to Colorado's. This part of the garden thrives without any supplemental irrigation.

The narrow corridor along the west side of the house is home to a moody garden, a sultry blend of red, purple, orange, and magenta colors. "This is where I like to flaunt the limits of color compatibility," she says. Marcia concedes that visitors often hurry by this area. "They don't seem to get it—but this is my favorite part of the garden."

Rock gardens and beds of sun-loving flowers encircle the small lawn and patio behind the house. Pockets of shade are starting to develop under the few maturing trees and these are stuffed full of woodland flowers. But change is as inevitable as the succession of September snow storms on the plains of Colorado. Many trees are knocked down before they have an opportunity to grow, so this garden is never the same two seasons in a row. The Tatroes wouldn't have it any other way. They see every disaster as a reason to try something new.

Lakewood

From the start, Eileen and Patrick Mangan's garden was never their own. In May 1988, Eileen began the process of converting a greenbelt outside her and brother Patrick's Lakewood apartment complex into a garden the size of a small soccer field. With the help of friends, she moved tons of topsoil onto the barren, rock-filled space, and lugged stones from nearby fields to make paths across the natural hill. "Then we started planting—mostly zinnias and marigolds from the grocery store," says Eileen. "But people got excited to see the garden take shape, and strangers and passersby would leave us geraniums and petunias to add to the garden."

The apartment manager did not catch the general gardening excitement. With requests for a watering hose denied, Eileen was reduced to watering her fledgling plants by hand. Just as her energy was flagging, Patrick and his friends got the gardening bug. The group rototilled the entire area, and Patrick, a fine arts botanical photographer, used his artist's eye to contour the hill into a pleasing slope with niches for specific garden areas. Boulders and rocks were rolled onto the slope for visual interest, and one friend spent a day digging irises from his fields to transplant into the newly reinvented garden space. More friends donated rose bushes, benches, and trellises, and made wooden signs to direct visitors around the ever-expanding site. A new apartment manager not only installed hoses for watering the garden, but built retaining walls of timbers and riverbed rock to surround the slope of the garden's perimeter.

And then the real trouble began.

"By 1995, we had created a massive garden park of flowers, shrubs, and trees. The garden was a photographic backdrop for couples about to get married and students graduating from high school. Families would picnic there and friends would meet to hang out," says Patrick. "And then the city called. They had decided to build a bike path that would go straight through our garden, and that was going to be that."

After many urgent phone conversations, the city engineer finally agreed to tour the site. Walking through drifts of cosmos, phlox, lilies, and irises, past trellises packed with morning glories, clematis, sweet peas, and silver lace vines, and through woodland areas shaded by Russian olive and redbud trees, the engineer converted to the Mangan garden cause.

"The engineer had the city reroute the bike path twice to save the garden," says Eileen. "Finally the path was reconfigured to wind between the edge of the garden and Bear Creek that flows beneath it. It's a much better plan than the original one."

Garden areas named after friends, cats, and the stumps of trees fill the crescent-shaped garden space. In the Owl Garden, 'Black Prince' snapdragons, 'Mahogany' nasturtiums, and bright red cardinal flowers cluster around a stump with owlish features. Apricot hollyhocks and salmon poppies ramble among blue clouds of Russian sage in Bertha's Garden, where a sturdy log invites visitors to rest a bit. Groucho the Cat, a neighborhood pet, has inspired a garden of yellow irises, daisies, coreopsis, and white lilies that mimic the textures of his coat. In the

Columbine Garden, wallflowers, chives, and white poppies set off a variety of yellow, red, and blue columbines grown from seed. Swirls of tiny white baby's breath blossoms surround the pinkish-white spires of Husker Red penstemons and spikes of purple irises in a garden area devoted to Joseph, a beloved cottonwood stump.

"It's been quite an adventure," says Eileen, a home health-care nurse. "I look from my balcony and see people literally falling off their bikes when they cycle past the garden. Often, I go down and talk to people about what we're trying to do."

And what is that?

"It used to be a secret garden before the bike path," she explains. "Now it's a public garden. Patrick and I feel a responsibility to inform visitors about the variety of native plants that will thrive in our region."

Secret no more, the Mangans' extended family-friend-neighborhood garden is a city treasure and hopeful inspiration for more "unowned" gardens to come.

Lakewood

As a young boy, Gordon Koon knew he wanted to spend his life growing things. He planted his first garden with his mother at the family's Denver home. His favorite plants from that garden—a collection of hybrid bearded irises—accompanied him to college and graduate school where he received horticultural degrees. The irises went with him when he opened a carnation nursery in 1950, and again when he began the Englewood Garden Center in 1972, a nursery south of Denver known for its wide selection of perennials and drought-tolerant plants. To the chagrin of area gardeners, Gordon closed the Englewood Garden Center in 1997. Once again, he packed up his irises and planted them in the garden behind his home in Lakewood, west of Denver.

A plaque reading "Old gardeners never die, they just spade away" greets visitors to Gordon's backyard haven. Across a steep hillside, basket-of-gold, creeping phlox, and woolly and Turkish veronicas alternate in glistening carpets of golden yellow, pink, and purple. Pansies, Corsican violas, and sedums tumble through the plantings along with anemones, foamflowers, pasqueflowers, and fall asters. Scattered between the plants are rocks and flat stones, home to more ground covers and other spreading plants. "I use the rocks as my work platforms. Their size and shape determines what I will plant there," says Gordon.

In a shady corner of the yard, the pale green fronds of four-foot ostrich ferns mix with the arching, leafy stems of Solomon's seal among hostas, Lenten roses, and wild ginger. The flowers of forget-me-nots, columbines, and bright pink and purple primroses sparkle among the lush foliage.

Ruffled pink and yellow azalea blossoms with four-inch diameters highlight Gordon's perennial bed. Unusual in Colorado gardens, Gordon claims that the acid-loving plants (he favors the hardy 'Exbury' hybrids) will grow in soil amended with sphagnum peat moss.

Huge red oaks, maples, white pines, and spruces from an old neighboring estate border the Koons' yard, and views of Mount Evans appear over the tops of the trees.

Gordon loves every part of his yard, but the bearded irises still stop him in his tracks. "What could be prettier?" he asks.

Englewood

Gourmet cooks Donna DeSimone and Steven Brenman spend nearly as much time in the kitchen as in their garden. The couple began with a vegetable garden in 1983, adding something new every few years. "We've got horses," explains DeSimone. "We needed something to do with all that manure."

Visitors to their home in Cherry Hills Village are greeted at an entry courtyard created by the U-shape of the house. Brick paths divide the area into four beds, each lined by clipped red barberry hedges encircling lavender and fragrant pink 'Sheer Elegance' roses.

Just a few steps from the kitchen door lies the vegetable and herb garden. Oft-used favorites include basil, tender French pole beans, hot peppers, Oriental eggplant, and sugar snap peas. DeSimone uses lavender throughout the house, even stuffing some in daughter Christina's and her husband's pillows. "Steven asked me what those weeds were in his pillow," she recalls, "but we really do sleep better in summer now."

Brick edging helps to contain aggressors like lemon balm, mint, and chives. Flowers for cutting and drying to make winter wreaths are also integrated into this bed, which surrounds a red potting shed crisply trimmed in white.

Perennial beds, punctuated by lichen-covered boulders, curve around blue spruce and clumps of aspen. Their ivory bark is complemented by pink Japanese anemones, low-growing *Lamium maculatum* 'White Nancy,' white ground cover mums, and ostrich and Japanese painted ferns.

A two-streamed waterfall cascades down boulders into a pool where koi dart beneath cattails, Japanese irises, and water lilies. Iceland poppies, creeping phlox, and more irises grow in the crevices above the waterfall, while purple clematis drapes across the rocks. The family enjoys the soothing sound and watching the birds the water feature attracts. "Even in winter," says Steven, "we enjoy the view of it from our green-house with orchids blooming around us."

Anne Weckbaugh

Englewood

After many years of gardening in Denver, Anne Weckbaugh still lights up remembering the start of her gardening career.

"I was a young wife and had just moved to the country in Cherry Hills, when landscape architect Persis Owens and Rebecca Enos, another avid gardener, asked me to join their women's group. It was a fascinating mix of women—all much older than myself and all very accomplished. This was during World War II, so we went to each others' houses and darned socks and made things for the war effort while we chatted. We always ended up talking about victory gardens and for some reason about onions, so we called ourselves 'The Onion Set.' Persis told us about a new way of gardening—creating landscapes that looked natural and reflected the beauty of the Rocky Mountain region. She was my inspiration. After that I was hooked."

Anne was also influenced by George Kelly, who wrote *Rocky Mountain Horticulture Is Different*. This groundbreaking work provided the first solid and specific information for Rocky Mountain gardeners and endures as a valuable resource today. In 1943, Anne joined a group that Kelly and others formed to promote a horticultural outlook specific to the region, the Colorado Forestry and Horticulture Association (CFHA), the precursor to the Denver Botanic Gardens. Meetings were held in a Victorian home donated as the organization's first headquarters by Gladys Cheesman Evans, a member of two prominent Colorado families. Since demolished, the house stood near Civic Center, around the corner from where the Denver Art Museum now stands. Anne remembers the excitement of planning the first botanic garden at City Park, and of establishing permanent headquarters and gardens at the present York Street site. Denver Botanic Gardens, Inc. (DBG) was founded in 1951, and George Kelly was the first editor of *Green Thumb Magazine* (now entitled *Mountain, Plain, and Garden*), still the official magazine of DBG.

"George had a nursery on South Santa Fe, and I practically lived there," says Anne. "I was fascinated with the different varieties of plants that he carried. I learned gardening techniques from him as well: the idea of watering in, or saturating the sides of a hole with water before planting, and also the concept of double digging, or shoveling a planting hole to a depth of two spade lengths then adding at least one-third organic material. Once I watched George double dig a seventy-five-foot-long trench for chokecherry shrubs. He used a Sharp Shooter spade and it took him hours, but those shrubs really took off."

Anne's gardening zeal inspired her to create gardens at both her own home and at her parents' residence in Englewood, south of Denver. Anne and her family eventually moved there, bringing plants, trees, and shrubs from their original home. Standing among the towering bristlecone and Scotch pines, white firs, and black walnut trees that she planted in 1954, Anne muses about the challenges she faced in developing low maintenance landscaping for the site. "This was a worthless piece of land when my father bought it, and nobody else wanted it. Because it lay beneath the High Line Canal, some of the area was marshland. Under the house and the surrounding land were sandstone and rocks. There were no other houses around for miles—except for Myron Blackmer's estate, now Kent Denver School."

Today Anne's house and gardens and the empty fields behind them are an oasis in the middle of a well-populated residential neighborhood. In the courtyard at the home's entrance stands a redbud tree with four trunks growing from its base. The branches of the redbud extend through the center of the courtyard's lattice roof. Ferns, mountain bluebells, pincushion, and purple fringe flowers cluster around the tree in the dappled light.

A gate leads to the side yard, a long rectangle of lawn lined with perennial beds. Blue and purple anemones mix with poppies and white tulips under a goldenchain tree in the upper garden. Along the opposite fence, 'Casa Blanca' lilies stand in full-blown perfection. Anne claims that applying the slow release fertilizer Osmocote in the spring assures

huge, long-lasting blooms. Under the firs and pines at the end of the yard grow papery blue love-in-a-mist, violets, and pansies. Rounding the corner to the backyard is a bed filled with daylilies and dwarf irises, and a garden of tree peonies with huge yellow, lavender, and pink flowers. A bur oak backs up the medley of color and shapes in this informal part of the garden.

Anne is always on the lookout for new and interesting plants. In an enclosed pool area to the side of the house are passion vines, silk oaks, and Italian stone pines that she has collected from her travels. Anne winters over delicate plants from her garden in the protected space, and baby-sits plants for friends and fellow plant fanatics as well.

Past the pool house, stone steps lead down a small hill to the backyard gardens. Unusual trees like smoke tree with its purple haze of blooms, Kousa dogwood, native to Korea, and fringe tree, which blooms in profuse clusters of lacy white flowers, grow among viburnum and daphne shrubs on the slope. More ornamental trees and shrubs spread around a corner into the lower garden.

The lower garden is a heavenly space where many family weddings and special occasions take place. A wooden gazebo stands next to a pond that is inhabited by a tall bronze crane. To either side of the gazebo stretch wide beds of glorious perennials—lupines, delphiniums, daisies, salvias, coneflowers, phlox, peonies, tulips, stone cress, spurges, irises—all combined in a gay profusion of perfect symmetry and balance.

Anne takes two turns in her gardens daily, weeding and pruning along the way. Her lush and colorful landscape and her unwavering enthusiasm are inspirational to anyone interested in gardening on the plains.

Englewood

Linda Heller's love of the Desert Southwest is reflected in her garden in Cherry Hills Village. Her starkly contemporary home is modeled on the design of southwestern pueblos. It inspired her to surround it with plantings that evoke the mystique of the desert but with a Colorado interpretation. A collector of modern art and sculpture, Linda appreciates intense, bright color and strong line. The garden translates her sensibilities into living form and visually links the interior of the house with the outside.

Linda began the garden in 1992, knowing it would evolve with time. The site is relatively flat, but she sculpted the land to give it the rhythm of gently rolling hills. Of primary importance to her were the structure of evergreen and deciduous trees as well as rocks. She selected and placed those in the rock garden near the front entrance with meticulous attention. "I hauled them all home in the trunk of my car," she says. Hardy cactus and agaves set the tone for this area, and potted cacti, succulents, and desert shrubs surround the front door, where they contrast effectively with the white stucco walls of the house and a striking abstract sculpture. Simple white clay pots emphasize the architectural qualities of the plants they contain.

Curving beds flow around the house and extend to the property's perimeter, leaving stretches of green lawn that act as a soothing counterpoint to the vivid flowers. Heller works with designer Tom Peace to create brilliant combinations that look great over an extended period. "Linda isn't afraid of color," Tom says, "but she also values the strength and subtlety of foliage plants to showcase it effectively." Linda's passion for ornamental grasses ensures strong vertical lines, interesting textures in every season, and nearly perpetual motion.

The grasses provide a unique structure on which to frame the perennial plantings. Perennials such as

Russian sage, purple coneflower, daylilies, and salvias are the mainstay of these beds, but annual additions guarantee that Linda can satisfy an ever-changing appetite for specific tones. Scarlet salvia, 'Homestead Purple' verbena, stately white woodland tobacco (*Nicotiana sylvestris*), and sunflowers contribute to the perennial borders. Carefully selected shrubs such as red barberry, rugosa roses, and chokeberry anchor the borders and provide strong backdrops to the flowers and grasses.

The jewel of the garden is the pond. Water adds dimension as it trickles down rocks into the upper basin and finally spills into the larger pond. "It's really the heart of the place, like an oasis," says Tom. "We made every effort to feature exciting perennials among the stonework around the pond, so that it's beautiful in every season and from every angle." Lushly planted with grasses, Joe Pye weed, specimen conifers, and ever-changing annuals, the rocky hillside provides a strong focal point from the west-facing patio. Striped cannas, irises, and water lilies add contrast and reflect on the water's surface. The sound and motion of the water feature also provides an effective juxtaposition to the desert-inspired plantings of much of the garden.

The slope behind the pond levels into a "native grass panel" evoking images of the prairie. The wispy silhouettes of grasses like little blue stem, prairie dropseed, blue grama, and needle-and-thread grass are delightful in every season. Dryland perennials such as Mexican hat (*Ratibida columnifera*), Indian blanket, black-eyed Susan, liatris, and flea bane daisy float above the sea of grass. The prairie area is beautiful even in winter when frost dramatically outlines the grass heads. The setting sun illuminates this panel and the pond from behind, creating nature's own abstract painting. Art lover Linda appreciates that.

Littleton

A sign in Mary Ellen and Bob Tonsing's green-house reads "Littleton Botanical Garden." Although the sign is intended as a joke—a gift from a friend—it's not far from the truth. The acre garden serves as a repository for an impressive variety of plants in a romantic setting.

Enclosed by a forest of deciduous and evergreen trees, the centerpiece of the garden is a white-painted gazebo, floating like an elegant ship in a sea of flowers. The gazebo was built in 1981 on the foundation of a "built-to-last" concrete fish pond that the previous owners had eventually filled with soil and crowned with junipers. Removing the massive shrubs proved to be challenge enough; demolishing the concrete seemed nearly impossible. The gazebo provided the perfect solution, serving as a focus of the garden and complementing the Tonsing's charming 1915 farm house. The gazebo is a favorite spot for entertaining guests and has hosted seven family weddings. In addition, it affords a 360-degree view of the plantings in the curved beds that flow around it.

Mary Ellen uses soft colors that show to advantage in the verdant setting. White, pale yellow, and lavender flowers dominate her sunny borders surrounding the gazebo, although a few bold strokes of golden yellow, peach, and crimson enliven the proceedings. Silver, bronze, and chartreuse foliage plants add drama. The plants themselves contribute to the lush, romantic feeling. Billowing shrub roses, graceful grasses, mounding hardy geraniums, and the stately spikes of foxgloves and foxtail lily evoke the feeling that many people associate with an English garden. The plants, however, are selected for their ability to thrive in this climate. Their good health—and Mary Ellen's artistic placement of them—create the romantic picture.

Much of the garden grows beneath a dense canopy of trees. "My biggest obstacle has been root

competition," says Mary Ellen. "Trees are greedy, especially spruce. You have to give the plants beneath them lots of compost and make sure they receive enough water—and be patient."

Although she was initially a reluctant shade gardener, Mary Ellen has fashioned a carefully orchestrated woodland garden that appears to be completely spontaneous. Understory shrubs (those that evolved in low light under trees) add structure and height in the shade garden and many offer colorful blossoms. Mary Ellen treasures dwarf hemlock, variegated kerria, false spirea, daphnes, thread-leaf birch, beauty bush, and the blue-leaf shrub rose, *Rosa glauca*. A ground-hugging dogwood, *Cornus canadensis*, a mere three inches tall, surprises visitors with its white blossoms at their feet.

Spring is particularly showy in the shady portions of the garden, with ephemeral blossoms of snowdrops, squills, and crocuses blooming in late winter, followed by spring daffodils, trilliums, and trout lilies. Perennials continue the show into summer in the filtered light. Many of them are selected for their outstanding foliage as well as their flowers, such as meadow rue, fringe cups, hostas, coral bells, Japanese anemones, many species of primrose, and the largest collection of ferns in the state.

About forty species of ferns grace the garden. So adept is she at growing ferns from tiny spores in her greenhouse, Mary Ellen has become known as the "Fern Lady" in gardening circles around the world. Among her favorite species are the elegant maidenhair fern and a rare red-stemmed fern she received as a gift from the Moscow Botanic Gardens —a fitting tribute to a woman who was once daunted by the prospect of making a garden beneath her trees. "Shade is not a liability," says the proprietor of the Littleton Botanical Garden. "It's an opportunity."

Littleton

After more than four decades of working on his hands and knees in his Littleton garden, Reed Johnson still looks forward to the excitement of spring. At seventy-six years of age, however, he jokes about the effects each passing year has on his gardening. "I spend a lot of time on my knees praying that I can get up again," he says.

Reed's love for the earth and growing plants has a long family history. As a boy, he helped his mother garden on the family's 365-acre Shadycroft Farm in Littleton, named by Reed's grandparents. The farm was worked by the Johnson family from 1903 until 1948, when all but fifteen acres were sold by Reed's father. Reed and his wife Tee built a house on those remaining acres in 1956 and, to carry on the family tradition of preserving and improving the land, began landscaping the yard—then nothing more than pasture with a single cottonwood tree and a pond.

As he collected ideas for the new yard, he found himself at a local greenhouse, the Cottonwood Shop, owned by George and Sue Kelly. The Kellys were among the first landscapers in Colorado to advocate the use of native plants, and they advised Reed and his wife on the development of their original plan for an English garden with pools, streams, and trees. The result is a blending of plants and styles achieved, in part, by what Tee calls her husband's "natural sense of what looks right."

"What I enjoy most is designing small garden areas and then merging the areas together into a natural-looking whole," says Reed. To achieve this seamless look, Reed takes a Polaroid photo of the existing garden and paints in the features he wants to add.

Today Reed and Tee enjoy their tranquil yard with its expansive lawn sloping from the patio to the pond. The pastel blooms of perennials and roses surround a white gazebo, and a winding stream borders the shade gardens. The stream originates from a series of pools that start at the edge of the patio by the house and meanders around plantings of forest-green junipers and rust-colored barberry shrubs. The water trickles over rocks at the base of ponderosa pines underplanted with white and lavender meadow rue, blue hostas, and the soft pink flowers of fern-leaf bleeding hearts. As the stream flows downhill, shooting stars, marsh marigolds, and trilliums crowd under the shade of native trees and shrubs.

In early summer, Johnson blue geraniums, purple irises, pink roses, and lavenders bloom among the soft purple foliage of sea kale in the sunny borders of the gazebo. Contrasting spikes of pink and red lupine mix with Jupiter's beard and maroon pincushion flowers. At the edge of the patio facing the pond are three conical shaped euonymus shrubs growing side by side; Reed calls them his personal mountain range. Their unusual form give the shrubs a regality in contrast to the nearby plantings of columbine, catchfly, fairy roses, and creeping phlox, and their peaks direct the eye to the view of the yard and, farther, to the bevy of swans floating in the pond.

Reed reflects on his years of landscape planning, planting, rock placement, and stream building with the modesty of a seasoned gardener. "It seems that both the garden and I have finally matured," he says. "Unfortunately, as it appears to me, the garden has ended up looking a good deal better than I do."

Littleton

When it comes to gardening, Carrie and Mike McLaughlin don't agree on much, which is why they've agreed to separate gardens. While Mike leans toward a rocky, green-hued aesthetic, Carrie loves flowers and splashes of color. What they did agree on was to tear up the flat manicured lawn that surrounded their Littleton home. In its place, Mike designed a flowing landscape of rocky berms, tree-shaded hillsides, orchards, and water features. Borders of perennials and native plants flow across the three-quarter-acre property that overlooks the green expanse of Jefferson County Open Space and the mountains beyond.

Inspired by the plateaus of northwestern Colorado, Mike built a rock watercourse, which he calls Arroyo Walk. This is his favorite part of the garden, where ground covers spread among rocks and drought-tolerant trees and shrubs. "People get lost in the bloom, but the quality is in the leaf," he says. In a landscape reminiscent of Moorish tile work, large and small puzzle-shaped areas of ground cover flow under larger shrubs and trees. Patches of fine-leafed dwarf thyme and hen and chicks intermix with carpets of intensely fragrant garland daphne (a spreading, evergreen shrub) under Montgomery spruces, an ivy-leafed turbin oak, and Mike's cherished 'Carol Mackie' daphnes with their gold-edged leaves.

As Mike's garden blends into Carrie's, the greens give way to brightly colored flowers. Carrie is especially fond of yellow loosestrife juxtaposed with June-blooming irises, and the dark purple-blue flowers of monkshood shining against the autumn colors of Pagoda dogwoods, Arctic willows, Korean barberries, and 'Shubert' chokecherries on her aptly named Shrub Hill.

Another favorite area is Kinnikinnik Hill, a shady garden close to the house that harbors Carrie's tree peonies flowering in extravagant dinner-plate-sized blooms.

"I try to keep her from planting in my garden and she tries to keep me out of hers, but sometimes we get into each other's spaces," Mike says. It is just this playful spirit of competition that keeps the McLaughlins' expansive gardens diverse and ever-changing. They do, of course, appreciate each other's gardening styles and find the most pleasure in sitting on a rustic bench in the grassy southwest corner of the yard after a long day of gardening, taking in the mountain view with a glass of wine.

Marilyn Raff

Littleton

Designer Marilyn Raff isn't a slave to her Littleton garden. "I garden when I feel like it," she says. Judging by the look of the perennial borders, shade garden, and two rock gardens, she feels like it a lot.

"I love making combinations that look great throughout the seasons—even in winter," she explains. "It's like designing a dance between the plants and the solid forms of the rocks." The diversity in her garden provides an always-changing panorama. "A garden changes so rapidly, week to week, that it seems like we have more than four seasons in Colorado," Marilyn observes.

One of the hallmarks of her design is combining shrub roses and grasses in context with perennials. The linear grasses complement the sprawling roses. In addition, rose hips contrast effectively with tawny grass blades in autumn and winter. One of her favorite combinations is the coral pink shrub rose 'Ferdy' combined with the smaller size maiden grass 'Yaku Jima.' The long-blooming perennials bloody cranesbill geranium and 'Butterfly Blue' pincushion flower planted at the base of the rose complete the composition.

Other shrub roses that Marilyn features in her garden and rates highly include 'Dortmund,' with single crimson flowers; 'Golden Wings,' which produces large, light yellow single flowers into October; and *Rosa rugosa* 'Alba,' with highly fragrant single white flowers and showy orange-red hips in autumn.

Marilyn never worries if things don't work out exactly as she planned, preferring to work with nature—and circumstances. "We moved most of the boulders in by hand for the rock gardens," she explains. "I had a preconceived notion of precisely how I wanted them placed, but the rocks wouldn't cooperate and my husband Jeffrey got frustrated. The final design of the rock gardens is based on a spur-of-the-moment decision to save my marriage."

Littleton

Tina Jones' garden is for the birds. And the butterflies. And the wildlife. "I started out with an acre of weeds, bluegrass, and six trees," recalls Tina. She decided to create the disappearing habitat that attracts birds and butterflies, including short, mid, and tall grass prairies.

"Because of my plantings, I'm getting state records for birds nesting in my garden," says Tina, a botanist, ornithologist, and wildlife consultant/teacher. August and September are peak months in her Littleton garden, with the non-stop bloom of rabbitbrush, Apache plume, plains goldenrod, fern bush, Russian sage, butterfly bush, blue mist spirea, and desert four o'clock (*Marbles multiflora*). Hummingbirds have made themselves at home, with average daily sightings of five to twenty birds from mid-July through the end of September. Tina is also thrilled by the arrival of migrating monarch butterflies.

Pathways of rough grass wander through the garden, often with tall prairie perennials towering on either side. This is no manicured suburban garden. Its apparent wildness, however, shouldn't be mistaken for lack of care. Tina carefully monitors plant populations, keeping the aggressive ones in check, and constantly rearranges for aesthetic reasons. "I've learned from my mistakes," she admits, "like planting some plants too close together." Tina also learned that nesting chickadees and house wrens take care of insect problems in the garden.

Some areas of the garden receive moderate irrigation, but most areas rely principally on natural rainfall. "Don't overwater!" emphasizes Tina. Native plants, as well as the animals they shelter and feed, thrive just as they would if "civilization" had never encroached upon the land. Tina feels passionate about providing a little piece of our natural vegetation to wildlife. "I love watching a northern oriole and her chicks clinging to the red-hot pokers in my garden, sticking their bills into each flower for nectar. It makes me feel good that I've created a safe place for them."

Angela Overy

Sedalia

The Colorado foothills are a far cry from the English countryside where Angela and Hugh Overy were raised. The couple immigrated to this country in 1963, lived in Denver for twenty-five years, and eventually settled south of Sedalia. "We were drawn to the openness of the state, especially the mountains and expansive sky," explains Angela. "It's an always-changing, ever-fascinating spectacle. We built our home and garden so we could watch it every day."

A walled courtyard skirts the tile-clad stucco house. A tiered fountain splashes above native flagstone paving softened by thyme and pussytoes. Mexican terra-cotta pots hold bright explosions of lilies, verbena, and other annuals.

Angela, a botanical artist and gardening author, finds inspiration in the garden flowers and surrounding flora. Much of the garden is populated by native wildflowers such as penstemons, Indian blanket, and sulfur flowers that thrive under the brilliant sunshine, although growth is compact and slow due to nearly constant wind. Angela augments the perennials with a series of bulbs that bloom throughout the season.

Outside the garden walls, the plantings meld into the natural landscape. "Some visitors might expect to find a pastel English garden," Angela says, "but that's exactly what we didn't want. There's no lawn here, and brighter flowers reflect the colors of a hot climate."

Feeders and houses attract many birds, such as insect-eating blue birds, seed-eating gold finches, and nectar-drinking hummingbirds, which feast on the scores of red flowers. Except for the decorative wall near the house, there's been no attempt to fence out wildlife from the property. Rainwater is diverted from the gutters of the roof through a series of pipes to the garden and a stock tank that offers a cooling drink to elk and deer. The animals seem to repay the kindness by refraining from nibbling on most of the garden.

Black Forest

"When it's the last day on earth we'll still be gardening," says Laura Spear.

This is not an idle threat. Tim and Laura live on five acres in rural Black Forest, northeast of Colorado Springs. Their ranch house is engulfed by the gardens that surround it. They named their gardens Forest Edge because the property is situated on the edge of the area's ponderosa pine forest. Across a meadow in back of the gardens, ponderosas frame a sweeping view of Pikes Peak. Red-tailed hawks and golden eagles sail across the idyllic landscape with regularity.

Laura and her husband Tim have found what they love to do, and their overflowing gardens of perennials, annuals, vegetables, and herbs reflect their passion—and their expertise. An effective gardening team, Laura provides horticultural know-how, while Tim applies his carpentry and engineering skills to garden structures and innovations.

"Tim has an affinity for creating garden spaces and conceptualizing where things should go," says Laura.

"Laura is the heart of the garden," Tim responds.

The entrance to the Spears' gardens is through the Moon Gate, an imposing structure that Tim fashioned from red oak and cedar. The oval doors set in a rectangular frame open to a backyard space filled with multicolored flower beds floating like islands among a system of cedar-chip paths. Rose campion, pink yarrow, coneflowers, phlox, and black-eyed Susans mix with hollyhocks and roses in gay profusion in the cottage garden-style beds. Godetias in hues of pink, white, and lilac are everywhere. The satiny annuals spill over the pathways along with violas, alyssum, and dragon's blood sedums.

The pathways are compost-makers in disguise. Laura scrapes back the cedar chips to expose an army of earthworms twisting through the rich earth

beneath. "This is Tim's idea," she says. "Dig a foot deep where the path will go, then add ten inches of manure, and throw in coffee grounds whenever you think of it. Top it off with six inches of pine needles and wood chips, tamp it all down, and wait two years. Worms will decompose the matter for a rich mixture you can harvest and spread throughout your garden."

Laura's favorite part of Forest Edge is the sweet smell of white and rose-colored Oriental lilies and white ruffled Byzantine gladiolus wafting through the Fragrance Garden, which borders the back patio. Aromatic tuberoses in more tones of pink and rose stand among lemon balm and scented geraniums, while spicier fragrances come from pineapple and chocolate mints grown in terra-cotta pots. At the end of the Fragrance Garden, deep pink sweet peas twine up clematis vines massed across lattice fencing.

Rounding the corner of the house, redwood steps lead to gardens situated on a southeast-facing slope. The slope provides a warmer, protected micro-climate for growing plants usually found in more temperate zones. Tim built a greenhouse for over-wintering the most tender of Laura's plant experiments. Bright pink 'Alika' rose bushes, a Gallica variety, stand on either side of the path that winds past gray-green eucalyptus shrubs, sage, and lavenders. White cosmos and the lilac purple flower clusters of six-foot *Verbena bonariensis* (native to South America), make a striking combination in large planters along the slope. Hot orange Mexican sunflowers and the huge white trumpet flowers of datura shrubs mix to dramatic effect at the base of the hill.

Texture and shape are as important as color and fragrance to the Spears' garden concept. The ruffled purple foliage of sea kale borders feathery Queen Anne's thimbles and the arching canes and pink flowers of red-leaf rose in the Wildflower Garden. The brilliant lavender stems and spiked blooms of sea holly present a foil for frothy baby's breath in the Peakview Garden, where gloriosa daisies and rudbeckias roam among fountains of blue avena

grass. Making a flamboyant appearance among lilac and sumac shrubs is a huge ornamental rhubarb with thick green leaves and four-foot plumes of tiny, deep red flowers rising from its center.

Every July and August, the Spears open their gardens for public tours to benefit a local charity. No Colorado garden-lover should miss viewing the many splendors of Forest Edge.

Joan Donner

Colorado Springs

"Where in the world am I?" is an often-asked question in Joan and Bob Donner's garden. Some visitors feel they've entered a savanna in Kenya, others the Tuscan region of Italy. A few have even suggested a Taos hacienda. However they experience it, everyone feels the mystique and drama of the outdoor space Joan has created.

"The garden is an outdoor extension of my home," says Joan. "I love texture, rich color, and surprising and unusual combinations. I like a little eccentricity, too."

The Donners' home is a 1927 Spanish colonial, designed by Chicago architect David Adler. Located on a windy bluff in Colorado Springs, the salmon adobe structure commands sweeping views of the surrounding countryside. The interior space of warm, deep colors and artfully arranged objects opens to a wide veranda and gardens where the play of unusual colors, plants, and garden features combine in a world that seems artless, yet perfectly conceived.

Silhouetted against the sky, four bronze cheetahs stare regally across a pool and brick courtyard at anyone entering their garden domain. A fountain and lily pond guarded by pampas grass occupy the center of the courtyard, and four apple trees packed with ripe, red fruit circle the area. Against a stucco wall to one side, Harry Lauder's walking stick, a small tree with fantastically contorted branches, grows with a pair of weeping mulberries among purple hollyhocks, Russian sage, irises, poppies, and delphiniums. The arching canes of hardy red-leaf rose cover the far end of the wall. Packed with flat dark pink flowers in summer and bright red berries in winter, the climbing rose is the type of plant with all-season interest that Joan favors. During winter months, the striking

shapes of trees and shrubs extend the beauty of the Donners' gardens well through the winter months.

Siberian pea trees, thorny shrubs with branches that fall fountain-like to the ground, and spreading yew and euonymus shrubs grow along flagstone steps that descend to gardens at the southeast side of the house. Under red cedar, larch, and juniper trees, a rustic table composed of a huge slab of sandstone mounted on top of four cedar trunks sits among the leafy textures of ferns, hostas, and Chinese rhubarbs. A variety of heaths and heathers grow along the wall that circles the area. "These are wonderful plants for all-season interest," says Joan. "They flower in pinks, whites, and yellows through the summer, and then their leaves turn from slate blues and deep greens to rich burgundy colors in the fall. In February, beautiful little white harebell flowers appear."

The gray-greens and silvers of native plants contrast with the rosy tones of the house along a hot, south-facing terrace. Sage, Apache plumes, Scotch brooms, and juniper shrubs grow among spikes of blue fescue grasses, and blend with the wild grasses and piñon pines crowding the terrace from the surrounding hillside. Clay pots brimming with fragrant herbs, succulents, and cacti are scattered across the flagstone surface, and lemon thyme creeps between the crevices of the stones. As she looks out over the plantings to the blue mass of Cheyenne Mountain in the distance, Joan confides this is her favorite garden area.

To the east, a forest of ponderosa pines defines another distinct microclimate in the Donner's yard. Sweet woodruff carpets the area in fragrant, white flowers in the spring. During summer, rhododendrons and azaleas prosper in the acid soil enriched by dropping pine needles. Growing among the spreading shrubs of 'Manhattan' euonymus, the large glossy green leaves of bergenias complement the silver-spotted leaves of lungworts throughout the growing season. "Foliage is of primary importance to me," says Joan. "The colors, shapes, and textures of leaves add such lasting dimension and interest to a garden."

Hanging from the back walls of the veranda are large mirrors that reflect the interplay of color and texture from the garden. Joan and her family and friends spend many hours on the shaded porch immersing themselves in the magical environment.

"Once a friend was sitting out here at night. He said the lights of the city below us looked like sailboats, and he imagined we were really on a South Sea island," says Joan.

Perhaps there are some places—and gardens—that belong in a world apart.

Judy Wills

Colorado Springs

The gift of an iris began Judy Wills' gardening career. It was not an ordinary iris, but the prize-winning 'Chivalry' that the plant's hybridizer, her father-in-law, presented to Judy as a house-warming gift in 1970. There must have been magic in the plant, because the gardens that Judy created are anything but ordinary, too.

Judy and Matthew Wills' home sits on a ridge in southwest Colorado Springs. Firs, pines, and native shrubs surround the property, creating a deep green backdrop for their Spanish home and the gardens around it. Stands of maple and hawthorn trees that Matthew planted are scattered through areas facing the home. The shredding dark brown branch of a Russian olive tree angles over the front door.

Trees fill the backyard as well, creating structure and shade for the different garden areas. As old trees fall, Judy creates more gardens to fill in the empty spaces. Wide flower beds curve along the perimeter of the long, narrow yard that winds and rises gradually to a hilltop gazebo.

Judy describes her gardens as old-fashioned, with lots of unusual shade-loving and wet meadow plants mixed in with more standard favorites. 'Betty Prior' floribunda roses grow among phlox in sunny beds directly behind the house. Underneath a gnarled bur oak, a white tree peony and fern-leaved dropwort frame spikes of white veronica, pink poppies, and frothy astilbes. Masses of 'Berlinger Kleene' dahlias hold center stage in the planting. Judy likens the dahlias' translucent, pink blooms to water lilies, and she uses the flowers through-out her beds to add freshness and carry the eye to the other plants. Clumps of lemon yellow 'Moonbeam' coreopsis lead to what Judy calls the Middle Garden underneath a huge ponderosa pine.

A three-hundred-pound black bear was the Middle Garden's most notorious visitor. The Wills' surprised him one morning as he sat munching bags of lady bugs among yellow daylilies, 'Peaches and Cream' verbenas, and deep purple pansies. "He really seemed to enjoy the spot," says Judy. "He sighed when he saw us, got up slowly, and lumbered off without ever disturbing a plant."

No wonder the bear was put out. Through the blooms filling the Middle Garden, he must have spotted the enticing

Woodland Garden, an area shaded by scrub oaks, white firs, and blue spruce. Seven-foot-tall meadow rues line the path through the garden, which is carpeted in soft green Scotch and Irish mosses. Meadow rue is Judy's favorite perennial, and it appears throughout her flower beds. She loves the "heirloom" feel and airy, delicate look of the plant. Along with the meadow rues, there are fuchsia tuberoses standing three feet tall. Saxifrage, violets, and hybrid impatiens spread among flowering strawberries and cluster around the stone bench tucked at the end of the Woodland Garden. The lemon yellow-cupped flowers of globeflower, or trollius, pop up in the subtle blend of blues, grays, and purples that mark this area.

Shrubs bring dimension and fragrance to Judy's gardens. Lilacs pruned to reveal their trunks stand against a wall of the house. The clusters of sweetly scented lilac blooms hang over another beautiful combination of plants: purple monkshood and delphiniums standing among bleeding hearts, white and blue bellflowers, 'Bowles' Mauve' wallflowers, and trumpet-shaped, deep blue gentians. Daphne, Korean spice viburnum, and cinnamon clethra shrubs grow among willowy Helen's flowers (plants bearing deep rust-colored daisy-like blooms), delphiniums, white lilies, and pink yarrow in flower beds that continue through the yard. At the gazebo, the view of blooms floating beneath the canopy of trees is breathtaking.

Judy has many tips for maintaining healthy, pest-free plants without using chemical sprays. She adds liberal amounts of worm casings to peat moss for a mixture that aerates garden soil and adds nitrogen. Believing that bananas provide potassium for plants as well as people, Judy puts the peels around her rose bushes for vigorous growth and long-lasting blooms. She spreads systemic rose food around all of her plants to protect against aphids. Lady bugs are Judy's favorite pest deterrent, and despite the attraction of bears, she buys hordes of the bugs that fly throughout her gardens, and migrate to her neighbors' yards as well.

Judy believes that working among her plants and flowers connects her to something greater than herself. Her gardens reflect the talent, vision, and love of someone well-attuned to nature's pulse.

Colorado Springs

Former Governor Roy Romer called High Valley Farm the most beautiful place in Colorado. Many other visitors have also marveled at the sprawling gardens set among three lakes, creeks, and a forest of trees. With sweeping lawns between plantings, a large sunken patio, and statuary and fountains that appear in open areas and secluded nooks, the eight-and-a-half-acre site resembles the parkland one might expect to find surrounding a chateau. Instead, High Valley Farm is located in the middle of a residential area in Colorado Springs. Entering the property, low mountains rise into view across a lake bordered by ponderosa pines, enhancing the feeling of an oasis within a city and portraying a decidedly western landscape.

As well as its distinction for unparalleled beauty, High Valley Farm has an interesting history. It is the oldest homestead in the Pikes Peak region. The logs used to build the farmhouse in the mid-1850s are still visible at the base of the original structure. In 1925, Eugene Lilly bought the property. Lilly suffered from tuberculosis, and like so many other easterners migrating to Colorado, he hoped to regain his health in the region's pure, clear air. Seventy years later, Lilly had not only affected a cure, but developed his acreage into several thriving businesses. The property boasted a vegetable truck farm, a smokehouse for pheasants, and a trout hatchery. Lilly was renowned for the trout pâté he shipped to retail outlets across the country. When the Lillys sold their home and grounds in 1985, preserving and enhancing the property became a labor of love for many individuals.

Dusty and Gary Loo grew up in the neighborhood bordering the Lillys' place. They decided to buy the property as an in-town retreat for themselves, and a gathering spot for area cultural institutions and nonprofit organizations. Many benefits have been held at the site since the Loos' purchase.

When the Loos started work on their new property, it was a wilderness of native trees and shrubs that obstructed the mountain views and crowded around the lakes and streams. They asked Judy Sellers of Ptarmigan Landscape Design to transform the area into a more open and gracious setting.

"This has been a landscaper's dream," says Judy. "At High Valley Farm I have the growing conditions and the space to create a living collage of trees, shrubs, and plants that is constantly changing and evolving." Judy's first task was to clear out deadwood, vines, and unhealthy plants to create space, open up views, and bring a flow to the landscape. She used the expansive acreage to install mass plantings of bulbs, perennials, trees, and shrubs for dramatic sweeps of color, texture, and shape. In the spring, four thousand tulips, daffodils, and crocuses burst into vibrant color across the property. Twenty varieties of primroses cluster along the creeks fed by High Valley's natural spring. Among huge ponderosa pines, white firs, and blue spruce, Judy planted Japanese maples. Stone lanterns placed at intervals among the trees and beside the creeks and the delicate, many-stemmed maples give an Asian feeling to areas of the property. "With its evergreens, rocks, streams, and mountain vistas, Colorado does share a certain affinity with the landscape of Japan and parts of Asia," says Judy.

Located between the ponderosa pine forest of the Black Forest to the north and the piñon-juniper woodland of Fountain to the south, the Colorado Springs region has many diverse ecosystems. Because High Valley Farm is located in an alluvial plain at the base of the Pikes Peak Range, sediments from mountain streams have produced rich, two-foot-deep topsoil. Judy takes advantage of the growing environment and the microclimates along the creeks to introduce varieties of plants that might not ordinarily survive Colorado's climactic extremes. Louisiana irises, native to the Mississippi delta, bloom in coppery reds, blues, and purples along the edges of the central lake. Marsh marigolds, with heart-shaped leaves and cup-shaped silvery white and yellow flowers, grow among delicate white and pink shooting stars along creeks and lake banks. Tree peonies smothered with ten-inch bowl-shaped flowers shelter white-veined 'Baltica' ivy and the nodding purple-blue flowers of

bush clematis. Unusual trees growing at High Valley include redbud trees, vine maples, and saucer magnolias that produce saucer-shaped pink blooms measuring six inches across.

Placing flowering plants together with an eye for sequential bloom and continuing interest is key to Judy's gardening philosophy. Surrounding the trees at High Valley Farm are flower beds filled with color and texture. One of Judy's favorite areas is a cottage garden where a variety of daylilies bloom throughout the summer in yellows, apricots, whites, and mauve-pinks. The daylilies are interplanted with larkspur, and Judy says the two aggressive plants keep each other at bay in this spectacular, easy-maintenance bed. 'Magic Fountains' delphiniums, a midsized variety, and 'Alaska' Shasta daisies bordered by 'Lemon Gem' marigolds make another pleasing combination. Judy plants cosmos among the delphiniums so that the cosmos foliage takes over as the delphiniums die back. In a neighboring bed, the foliage of 'Pink Beauty' poppies shields the fading clusters of white lace flower blooms in August.

Perhaps Judy's favorite plants are daphnes, and varieties of the broad-leaf evergreen shrubs are scattered throughout the property. She favors 'Carol Mackie,' a medium-sized shrub with gold-edged light green leaves and clusters of pale pink flowers in spring, and the larger 'Somerset' that blooms in white flowers. "These plants have it all—structure, striking foliage, colorful blossoms, and wonderful fragrance," she says. "They make a wonderful backbone for any garden."

The gardeners who tend High Valley Farm have their own favorite plants and areas, and their own stories to tell. A close-knit group of friends and gardening fanatics has emerged from the employees hired to maintain the property. They host annual reunions at their homes and trade anecdotes about the garden sanctuary they have come to love. Avoiding the attacks of Scrappy the Swan, an ornery resident of the central lake; enjoying the antics of Porky the Duck who wanted to be a swan (he waddled about the property with his neck stretched out); and shoveling lion manure from the Cheyenne Mountain Zoo around trees to deter nibbling deer are only some of the unusual experiences they relate. Most of all, they enjoy reflecting on the pure joy of working in such a beautiful environment.

"It affects everyone," says Ceacy Thatcher, a part-time gardener at High Valley since 1987. "I watched a group from a nursing home having tea on the patio overlooking the lake and the view of Pikes Peak. When they got up to leave, they looked like different people from when they came in. They stood straighter, and held their heads higher."

A Colorado treasure, High Valley Farm is also a magical place that defies the boundaries of location, ownership, even logic. No one can quite explain why green parrots, native to Central America, occasionally fly overhead, or why so many exotic plants can grow there. High Valley Farm is simply a wonder and a tribute to all those who have helped shape its unique beauty and character.

▲ Primrose, marsh marigold, and ligularia

Colorado Springs

Prudence Walker thinks the love of gardening is an inherited trait. She remembers well her parents' garden, and now her own children are gardening addicts, too.

Because she gardens behind her Colorado Springs home, Prudence has a major challenge to overcome—the inevitable hailstorm that will batter her flowers to a pulp. Situated on the east side of Pikes Peak, Colorado Springs is susceptible to temperature inversions that dump eddies of cold air into the valley below. At anytime during the summer months, area gardeners can expect hail. "It's all right," she says. "I have to have my impatiens, anyway, so I plant whatever I want and live with what happens. A month after the hailstorm, my garden usually looks better than ever. It's fun to revive it."

Prudence's garden reflects her happy and exuberant spirit. A stone mermaid sits on a rock surveying the small backyard pool. Surrounding the pool, sweeps of color from carefully massed annuals and perennials flow among large boulders. White alyssum and deep pink impatiens edge plantings of the midsized 'Magic Fountains' delphiniums, followed by 'Husker Red' penstemons, white and salmon-colored nicotianas, and salvias. Topping the confection of plants are yarrows, daisies, verbenas, and Jupiter's beards. A swan planter filled with more impatiens twists its stone neck to view a variegated hosta at the edge of the pool area.

Although Prudence's husband Beno voted for a raspberry patch in the center of the yard, Prudence's design sense prevailed. The patch is at the back of the yard, and a pristine lawn is the cool center of the remaining garden areas. Close to the house, a plum tree with white clematis vining up its trunk shades mounds of moss rose. A border to the west is home to

butterfly bushes and creeping myrtle. In the spring, crocuses, daffodils, and irises poke through the dark green myrtle in a colorful display that reminds Prudence of the design on an Oriental rug.

At the south end of the yard, a stone lady wreathed in ivy welcomes Prudence and Beno's grandchildren to an adobe playhouse framed by hostas, bergenias, and bleeding hearts. Outside lace-curtained windows, planters drip with verbena and impatiens. It is an ideal setting for children bound to grow up gardeners themselves.

Pueblo

Bill and Karen Adams were happy simply collecting mushrooms in their spare time when they met Panayoti Kelaidis. Little did they know how their lives would change. Curator of the Rock Alpine Garden at Denver Botanic Gardens since 1980, Panayoti camped in the Adams' backyard while on plant-finding missions in the plains around Pueblo. An avid promoter of rock gardens and the garden potential of plants native to Colorado and similar climes, Panayoti inspired a new generation of these plants' enthusiasts. In 1993, as his newest convert, Bill retired from his banking career and joined Karen to start Sunscapes, a rare plant nursery.

In the Adams' front yard, a rock garden of colorful and unusual plants makes you a believer in the beauty of the plains. Low shrubs, small annuals, perennials, and bulbs cover the large mounded area in a tapestry of foliage and color that winds over and between assorted rocks. "Some of the plants are native to our region, and many come from steppe regions—like Turkey, Greece, South Africa—that have similar growing conditions to our own," says Bill.

Hot pink ice plants and bright yellow gazanias, both introduced from South Africa by Panayoti, carpet large areas of the Adams' garden. Rocky Mountain zinnias that grow wild around Pueblo provide sweeps of yellow color in spring. The mottled blue-green rosettes of the succulent *Aeoniopsis* invite closer inspection. *Penstemon angustifolius*, with sky blue tubular flowers, and showy oreganos with shrimp-like bracts enclosing pink flowers appear among daphne shrubs. The unusual prairie Indian paintbrushes bloom in spikes of pink, cream, and green flowers. Deep magenta African daisies and the plains native Blackfoot daisy, with its striking white blooms, grow at the front of the border with talinums, self-sowing annuals with magenta flowers perched on slender stems.

Blocks away, Karen landscapes exhibit areas at the Pueblo Zoo. Lions and tigers peer through zebra, ruby, and pampas grasses at red hot pokers and lion's tails, tender perennials with tiers of furry orange flower clusters grouped along their stems. As in her gardens at home, Karen proves that Pueblo and Africa are not that far apart.

$\mathcal{C}$olorado $\mathcal{M}$ountains

"Anyone crazy enough to garden in the mountains deserves the brilliant show of color that plants in the mountains produce," says Angela Foster of Basalt. Angela's cottage garden in the Roaring Fork Valley is filled with perennials and vines that bloom in the bright, crisp, long-lasting colors fostered by cool mountain air. Despite a shortened growing season, extremes of temperature, rocky clay soil, and the ever-present threat of foraging deer and elk, Colorado mountain gardeners like Angela find ways to meet the gardening challenges and to maximize the advantages. Their efforts are repaid with gardens of extraordinary beauty.

Colorado's Rocky Mountains, commonly known as the "roof of North America" because of its numerous 14,000-foot peaks, cover two-fifths of the state. Featured in this section are gardens at elevations from 6,000 to over 10,000 feet, bounded on the north by Steamboat Springs, the east by Evergreen, the west by Telluride, and the south by the San Luis Valley.

The refrain of "Amend your soil" is heard as loudly from Colorado's mountain gardeners as from gardeners in the plains and plateau regions. Creating berms of topsoil on top of the rocks and clay is a common practice in mountain gardens. In Carbondale, at the north edge of the Crystal River Valley, a gardener created mounded spirals of loamy topsoil for planting trees, shrubs, and perennials in her front yard. The spirals of plants encircle a private patio where this gardener enjoys her garden oasis in privacy as neighbors view the plantings from the street.

The prevalent rocks in mountain soil are used to advantage in many mountain rock gardens. After digging rocks out of their proposed garden site, a Steamboat Springs gardening team placed the rocks, plus boulders from nearby woods and meadows, on top of the steep front yard slope. In addition to creating a naturalistic setting for native shrubs, trees, and perennials, the rocks are a natural windbreak and provide microclimates where plants can thrive. Radiating stored heat, the sun-baked rocks make warm pockets of protected space around them.

"Tricking things into growing," as one gardener from Old Snowmass said, is a solid mountain gardening maxim. And taking advantage of existing growing conditions is as important as creating favorable, new ones. At 10,000 feet in Crested Butte, a seasoned gardener used the microclimate created by drainage water at the base of a berm to grow yellow monkeyflowers, wildflowers usually found in wet meadows at lower elevations. Stone walls, shaded arbors, and stream banks provide more environments conducive to growing specific plants.

Although most mountain gardeners complain of flower-hungry deer, the animals drive Evergreen gardeners to distraction. Finding novel deterrents seems a major town sport. One woman straps boom boxes attached to motion sensors into trees at the edge of her garden. When elk approach they activate the sensors, and the radio blares country music into the air.

With snow-capped peaks as a backdrop, mountain gardens have built-in drama and beauty. Meadows of wildflowers provide more inspiration. In a garden in Ridgway, near Telluride, flax, daisies, blanket flowers, and poppies jostle among aspen trees. Fireweed, Indian paintbrush, and scarlet gilia are a common sight in the meadows and gardens of Crested Butte; wildflowers like penstemons, larkspurs, and dame's rockets grow alongside Asiatic lilies in Vail and Breckenridge. Gardens in the Crystal River Valley town of Redstone boast huge deep blue delphiniums and three-foot-tall columbines that make puny impostors of the same plants grown anywhere else.

Some of the most lush mountain gardens are in the high country valleys. In the San Luis Valley, sweet peas tumble over fences, lilac shrubs line roadsides, and shrub roses, peonies, and blue mist spirea fill perennial borders. Buena Vista gardens burst with the vibrant blooms of lilies, veronicas, lupines, and Shirley poppies.

With all the challenges of gardening at high altitude, you could call mountain gardeners crazy. Viewing their gardens of dazzling beauty, however, might tempt you to join their ranks.

BUENA VISTA

Masonville

Making a new garden from scratch is a daunting challenge for any gardener. Lauren Springer accepted it when her family began to outgrow their home in Windsor, where her sophisticated cottage garden had received national acclaim. The lure of country living led the noted plantswoman and author to build a new home in a foothill canyon near the small town of Masonville, north of Loveland and near Horsetooth Reservoir.

The picturesque location for the house, which nestles in a protected spot surrounded by views of red stone canyon walls, provides a dramatic setting for the gardens. A year of earth-moving, thistle-killing, wall-building, and stone placement preceded planting, which began in earnest in 1997. "I lost all sense of gardening as a gentle art," recalls Lauren. "This was pure, brute force on a mammoth scale."

A square-walled courtyard, measuring eighty feet on each side, greets visitors on their approach to the warm-toned stucco house. A wooden walkway through the courtyard bisects the garden and leads to a rustic arbor covered by grapes, trumpet vine, and wisteria.

The clay-based soil, liberally enriched with organic matter, holds moisture well—an advantage when desiccating winds sweep through the canyon. Small trees, such as mountain ash, Western river birch, and purple-leaf May Day provide shade in the courtyard and offer flowers, fruit, and structure throughout the seasons. One half of this walled garden is devoted to warm pink, peach, and lavender-blue flowers, while the other half burns a bit brighter with orange, gold, and deep purple. Thousands of bulbs, including daffodils, squills, crocuses, and tulips start the spring show.

Shrub and perennial groupings, laced with annuals, also start early and erupt at regular intervals. Lauren judges plants not only for their flowers, but

for their strong constitutions and appearance even when not in bloom. She grows many from seed and ruthlessly composts them if they don't perform to her exacting standards. Favorite performers include ornamental grasses, kniphofias, and long-blooming natives such as prairie coneflower and Maximillian sunflower.

Outside the courtyard, a long stone walkway runs the length of the courtyard wall and continues past the house. It parallels a retaining wall that marks the beginning of the hillside garden. The plantings on the slope eventually merge with the natural vegetation, creating a seamless blend between the cultivated and wild plants. Lauren's distinct planting style, which echoes the patterns of natural plant groupings, also helps to blur the line where the garden ends and nature takes over. "I really go for plants with an untamed look—wild grasses, airy poppies, angular yuccas," she explains. Blossom colors on the hillside garden cover the entire spectrum; warm tones at one end gradually yield to cool hues at the other. Bronze and silver leaves alternately contrast and complement the drifts of flowers.

Structure in the garden is provided by the soft-set flagstone and tawny stucco walls, as well as selected architectural plants with four-season interest. "Dwarf conifers are my living statuary," Lauren says. "The froth of flowers that surround them is a fleeting thing, but the conifers give the garden depth and interest even in the dead of winter."

An additional aspect of the Springer garden is the jungle of potted plants. Clustered around doorways and displayed on patios, these container plantings tie the garden to the house. The plants offer dramatic forms that offer countless combinations from year to year, wintering over in a crowded greenhouse. Tender agaves, bamboo, cacti, succulents, and herbs bask in the summer sun and add to the sense of place.

Evergreen

Evergreen gardeners have grown to expect high winds and hail, and to expect to find decomposed granite in their flower beds, but their greatest challenge by far is protecting against the predawn raids by elk and deer.

To protect her naturalized cottage garden from the animals, Joan Reynolds has developed both practical and novel deterrents. Although the deer and elk love nibbling on her shrub roses and mountain bluet, they steer clear of more acrid plants like Munstead and Hidcote lavender, bee balm, and herbs. And hardy ground covers like woolly thyme withstand just about any tromping. She has also discovered that the spray plant food Bobbex is unpalatable to deer and elk. The product smells like sea kelp and adheres to the leaves and branches of ornamental plants even through rain and snow showers.

One of Joan's more novel tactics for thwarting deer is to tie motion-triggered boom boxes on trees. When neighbors hear loud country music blasting out in the middle of the night, they know Joan's out in her nightgown chasing away the pests with rocks. Such actions are the perfect example of her tenacious nature. She is "possessed," as she puts it, with gardening.

Hanging baskets and clay pots overflowing with her favorite annuals decorate the porches and deck of her Victorian-style home. Lobelia, pansies, sweet alyssum, scarlet flax, snapdragons, cleome, and striped *Malva sylvestris* all thrive in the cool mountain air. In June, tulips—deep rose-colored 'Queen of the Night' and ruffled pink 'Angelique'—bloom above the lacy white flowers of sweet woodruff in a large perennial bed at the center of the yard. Joan loves the glossy green leaves of the fragrant, hardy ground cover that spreads throughout her borders.

Her flower beds are so closely packed with plants that there's no room for mulching—or weeds. Planting bulbs would be impossible without another of her practical and unconventional remedies: she uses a four-inch auger on a power drill to create perfectly-sized holes for the bulbs without damaging the root systems of neighboring plants. "The drill even goes through small rocks," she says.

Perennial beds close to the house feature easy-care pink shrub roses complemented by blue mist spirea, giant alliums, Jacob's ladders, and the purple hues of spiderworts, lavenders, and dame's rockets. The yard slopes gently into a ponderosa pine forest to the south where native Indian paintbrush, columbines, penstemons, wild clematis, and sugarbowls bloom. Perennials lining the bluegrass lawn drift into the forest and mingle with the wildflowers.

Hundreds of wild bee balm grow on the north side of the house, and although Joan is not one for picking flowers from her garden, she says, "You could pick five bouquets, armloads wide, and not make a dent." It is a gardener's—and a photographer's—dream when the lavender-pink flowers bloom in August.

A professional seamstress, Joan schedules her sewing around the garden chores. With obvious gusto, practicality, and a seamstress' eye, she has created a near perfect blending of gardens and forest. Only the grazing elk and deer are missing.

Evergreen

"Composing a garden is like composing a picture," Gary Sohrweid says.

Gary is a painter. His acrylic works—painted on backgrounds of rich magentas, reds, and purples—feature landscapes with occasional old cars, vintage homes, and rooftops. His gardens reflect a similar aesthetic. Though he admires lush, manicured yards, Gary's affinity for both the abstract and the natural direct his gardening instincts. "I have learned to work with the land and not to force something totally different from what nature intended," he says.

The Sohrweids' home sits bordered by deep green forests on a slope in the middle of a four-acre aspen grove in Evergreen. Terracing the slope created flat tiers of earth for planting perennials and native plants. Gary remembers untold trips in his old Scout, dragging loads of topsoil and compost to make fertile garden soil out of the decomposed granite in his yard. More loads of rocks and boulders were used to line the terraces and control erosion on the slope.

Native plants such as trailing daisies, kinnikinnick, stone crop sedum, junipers, and firs fill the terraced gardens. Gary's pottery and garden art mix with farm implements at different points throughout the borders. "I find that the sculpture and art in the garden help me define who I am," he says. "I look at an object from every possible direction and decide if it fulfills a purpose by enhancing the setting."

Water recycles through an antique water pump, two vintage granite-ware kettles, and an old wash tub. This whimsical fountain sits on a low berm made of moss rocks behind a split-log bench. Sedums grow with daylilies in a kettle in front of the fountain. "I like the contrast of man-made objects next to natural vegetation," says Gary.

A few steps down a pebbled path on the north side of the house, tufts of blue fescue grass encircle a woodland nymph. The cement statue stands among the frothy white blossoms of sea kale. Wild strawberries clamber at the nymph's feet. From there a path lined with native Indian paintbrush, red flax, veronica, and an Austrian copper rose leads into the aspen grove.

When the Sohrweids' garden was chosen for the Evergreen Garden Tour in 1997, Gary wanted visitors to experience both his gardens and the natural beauty surrounding them. Not only did he lead nature walks through the woods around his home but he also mounted empty picture frames on poles in the aspen grove, inviting viewers to focus on their own aesthetic approach to nature. "Of course, there are always some people who don't get it," he says. "They just stick their heads through the picture frames and look confused."

Most people, however, do get it—the painterly approach balancing color, texture, and shape with a down-to-earth love of the outdoors—and the tour gave him a chance to directly communicate his instincts. "The frames inspire the feeling I've always wanted in the yard—the feeling of wandering through a natural painting."

Dodie Bingham

Breckenridge

"Something wonderful happens to me when I work in the garden, both physically and spiritually," says Dodie Bingham. "There is some magic chemistry between me and dirt. I love the digging, planting, weeding, and deadheading. I love the earth's smells and the colors of the flowers."

Something wonderful happens to everyone who passes Dodie's garden. Bounded by a low, weathered wood fence, the cottage garden occupies the small front yard of her shop, the Bay Street Company on Main Street in Breckenridge's Historic District. The shop is housed in the 1898 cottage of a gold prospector and his family. The tiny yellow flowers of potentilla bushes and the lavish orange and white blooms of Asiatic lilies spill through the fence and brush the knees of passersby. Waist-high wooden ducks standing guard at the central pathway beckon visitors deeper into a swirl of blooms. In the brilliant colors that only mountain air inspires, blue delphinium, yellow and pink foxgloves, and white cosmos dance among purple spires of veronica, lupines, peonies, columbines, irises, and bleeding hearts. Solemn wooden bears survey the flower symphony from the Bay Street Company's front porch.

"I start aerobics every spring to get ready for the garden," says Dodie. "It's hard work, but the rewards are incredible. People absolutely love it. They want to talk to me over the fence, so it's hard to get the work done, but that's okay. I feel a responsibility to create this beauty."

Dodie's life is a continuously blooming bouquet. Since moving to Breckenridge in 1978 and starting the Bay Street Company—a store specializing in interior furnishings, crafts, and accessories—two daughters have become partners in the thriving business. A son-in-law and grandchildren help with the shop and with the garden. They plant a thousand tulip bulbs every fall.

Planters brimming with multicolored pansies line the deck of Dodie's apartment above Bay Street Company. As she peers through the intense colors to the gardens below, she muses on her gardening passion. "The garden is my teacher, and I'm the caretaker," she says. "I don't control it—it controls me. The garden is where I lose myself, and where I find myself, too."

*B*reckenridge

Jane Hendrix thought she'd plant a few flowers outside her home-office window.

"They were so pretty I added a few more plants. Then I decided to extend the flower bed and then to create another bed. Pretty soon there were flower beds inching around the corner of the house and curving along the property boundary lines."

The rest is history. Many flower-filled raised beds, rock walls, and arbors later, Jane and her husband and garden co-conspirator Bob live in a paradise of extravagant, colorful blooms—although they last just six weeks of the year. Their house is near the Blue River in a subdivision just south of Breckenridge, a mountain community between Vail and Denver that stands at 9,500 feet in altitude. Snowstorms on the fourth of July, boulder-strewn clay soil, and winds that could make a blue spruce cry are only some of the conditions that keep the area's growing season so short. "It's worth it," says Jane. "The colors of the flowers are so crisp and vibrant here. The trick is to choose hardy plants that bloom at the same time—for a long time."

Drifts of solid color from the same species of plants are layered on top of each other throughout the Hendrix' flower beds. Outside Jane's office window, lines of purple pansies followed by the silvery whites of snow-in-summer border masses of pink, white, and red Oriental poppies that are backed by spires of deep blue delphiniums and lilac dame's rockets. A frothy mix of pink and white cosmos softens the vertical backdrop of plants. Continuing around the house, raised beds set in a well-manicured lawn are home to waves of yellow, red, and blue columbines, Icelandic and Himalayan blue poppies, purple bellflowers, and daisies.

The Hendrix' home overlooks Tenmile Range, and the edge of the property dips down into Arapaho National Forest. Thick stands of lodgepole pines surround the garden areas that continue through the backyard and culminate in the view of a garden swing surrounded by sweet William, foxgloves, and delphinium.

Featured in many gardening publications and a perennial favorite on the Breckenridge Garden Tour, the Hendrix' garden is an exuberant high altitude fantasy.

Breckenridge

Ask gardeners in Breckenridge about Jane Hendrix and her wonderful garden, and they will get confused —because there are two Jane Hendrix' that fit the description. Related only by their love of horticulture, the women live on opposite sides of town.

Like her neighbor to the south, this Jane Hendrix, who lives near timberline northwest of Breckenridge, loves to talk about gardening. But ask her the name of the sky blue, buttercup-like flowers spreading in her rock garden and she radiates pure joy. Not only can she tell you everything there is to know about the plant, but you have given her the opportunity to pronounce its name in Latin. "*Nemophilia menziesii*," she says. "I love how hard it is to say. The name tells you something about the plant, too. Since *Nemophilia* means 'grove-lover,' you can assume it will do well in shade." Commonly known as baby blue eyes, the annual is one of the many frost-hardy flowers that Breckenridge's "other" Jane Hendrix grows.

Less known than her famous namesake and friend, Latin-loving Jane has equally beautiful gardens that reflect a unique gardening outlook. Her first high altitude gardening attempts led her to extensive studies in botany, geology, chemistry, and soil science. "I began gardening in Illinois, where rocks are as rare as diamonds," says Jane. "When I moved to Breckenridge, I prepared my flower beds by sifting out all the rocks. When the spring rains came, the silky soil formed mud, then a hard crust, and the rain water ran right through it. All my plants died. Many library books later, I realized the rocks were holding moisture in the sandy soil. Now I actually add pea gravel to the topsoil when preparing a new bed."

Located in front of her home, Jane's garden consists of four large raised beds connected by gravel paths and bordered by aspen trees. The beds face north, south, east, and west and alternate between shade and sun throughout the day. In one bed, Siberian delphinium, a midsize variety with deep blue spires of flowers, and silvery lamb's ears grow with purple pansies and deep pink Aspen daisies among gray and white-streaked rocks. White clusters of dame's rocket and the white and pink bells of foxglove back 'Husker Red' penstemons, purple larkspur, and the ferny leaves of Jacob's ladders in a bed lined with mounds of basket-of-gold and purple rock cress. The large satiny flowers of red flax, a two-foot-tall annual, add splashes of brilliant color to the plant groupings.

Jane delights in small, unusual plants that poke up here and there and the mat-forming perennials that spread through the raised beds. Delicate fairy slippers, terrestrial orchids with fuchsia blossoms resembling tiny birds in flight, shooting stars, saxifrage, and two-inch-high 'Thumb Nail' hostas grace shady areas. Rich pink clusters of stone cress carpet sunny spots along with dwarf snapdragons, flowering in masses of mauve two-lipped blooms, and lilac geraniums with violet-blue flowers. Tucked against rocks are tiny cotyledons, succulents with fleshy leaves and tubular red flowers.

Every plant in the garden is identified—by Latin genus and species—on plant tags that Jane cut from the slats of vinyl venetian blinds. This is only one of Jane's many innovations, and one of the many ways that she shares her gardening knowledge with other high altitude gardeners. She opens her garden, named Mountain View Experimental Gardens, for self-guided tours during summer months. Jane also leads alpine walks that focus on studying wildflowers in their natural settings and adapting the information to residential garden conditions.

In her newsletter, *The High Country Gardener*, Jane describes frost-hardy plants and dispenses a variety of tips. For pest control, she encourages gardeners to plant German catchfly, a two-foot-tall perennial with a cluster of bright pink flowers and a sticky stem that "keeps any visiting insect stuck for good." More tips include filling raised beds below the first six to twelve inches (as far as most plants roots extend) with branches and stones to provide easier drainage, a rich decomposing base, and a cheaper way to fill the bed.

Jane will never complete all the projects she envisions in her garden—a place where time flies. "That's *tempus fugit* in Latin," says Jane.

To be Jane Hendrix of Breckenridge is to be a gardener who is one of a kind.

Barbara DeVoe

Vail

"Dear Garden Lady, My name is Paula, I am seven years old. And I really loved your garden! It's really pretty! Thank you for sharing your garden with me. Now that you shared your garden I will share our bread with you. P.S. I will bring the bread to you in a few days."

Barbara DeVoe found the note under a stone on her patio table, and sure enough, the bread arrived days later. The girl had visited the garden with her parents, owners of the Boulder Bread Company, following a tour of Barbara's gardens by the International Rock Garden Society. For the event, Barbara had built a path to the side of her property and posted a sign welcoming the group to her gardens. She forgot to take the sign down, and didn't notice that the public at large was touring the gardens as well. From that day on, the welcome sign ("Please come into my garden, my flowers want to meet you") has remained posted, and Barbara greets anyone straying into her gardens with warmth and enthusiasm.

It takes some effort to climb the steep, wooded hillside that surrounds the DeVoe home, but troops of daily summer visitors feel it's more than worth the effort. Shaded by aspens, firs, and acer maples, the slope is home to leafy hostas and comfreys, dwarf purple osier shrubs, and a variety of mints. Purple rock cress, sweet William, and pink dianthus spread over rocks and between ferns and clumps of lungwort, or pulmonaria, a low-growing perennial with lance-shaped, silver-spotted leaves. Foliage is important to Barbara, and layers of greens, grays, and silvers in varying shapes and sizes repeat among the flowering plants throughout her gardens.

At the top of the slope, the hill levels off into a gently sloping area behind the house. The area is flanked by layers of huge boulders interplanted with dense mats of flowering ground covers. Flagstone paths lead through borders where perennials and annuals mix with mugo pines, serviceberry shrubs, and foliage plants like lady's mantle, one of Barbara's favorite varieties. She loves the way water beads on the perennial's hairy gray-green kidney-shaped leaves and the haze of chartreuse blooms it produces. Among the mounds of lady's mantle, the silvery tones of 'White Nancy' lamium and sweet woodruff enhance the bright blue flowers of gentians. Furry balls of purple alliums and cone-shaped spikes of bluish-violet *Primula vialli* emerge at intervals from the mass of spreading plants. Frothy blue forget-me-nots race among lupines, coral bells, columbines, foxgloves, and delphiniums that fill the borders in a happy confusion of colors and shapes. Ruffled apricot parrot tulips paired with mounds of chartreuse euphorbia and deep blue monkshoods mixed with magenta and deep pink Asiatic lilies make striking plant combinations. As the garden area dips down closer to the house, prunellas, or cutleaf selfheals, with spear-shaped leaves and whorls of purple flowers, cluster among the large leathery leaves of bergenias along the walls of the foundation. "I think 'wild cottage garden' best describes this part of the yard," says Barbara.

On the other side of the yard, an underground spring surfaces and creates a boggy area. Barbara has taken advantage of the swampy conditions to plant marsh marigolds, trollius, and shooting stars among more bergenias. Forget-me-nots migrate through the plantings in a blue swirl that Barbara works hard to contain. Creeping veronicas and moss grow between flagstones that lead to a series of pools and falls. Barbara created the water feature by diverting the spring water down the hill on the opposite side of the house. Lamiums drip off rocks lining the pools, and columbines, trollius, primulas, and saxifrages tumble down the slope to the accompaniment of the falling water.

Birdhouses perched on walls and in the branches of trees indicate Barbara's live-and-let-live philosophy about the birds and critters that frequent her garden. "If you keep the wildlife fed, or at least let them be, they'll leave the flowers alone," she says. "A bear and her two cubs frequent the garden, and they are completely respectful of all the plantings. They never stray off the paths. When they're through sniffing and looking around, they just amble back into the woods."

Since 1976, Barbara and her husband have divided their time between their original home in Florida and their summer residence in east Vail. An orchid-grower during winter months, Barbara is completely in love with the wild beauty of her adopted mountain home and the varieties of hardy plants that thrive at 9,000 feet. A dirt path leads behind the house and cultivated gardens to Barbara's favorite garden area. Among aspen trees, native shrubs, grasses, and carpets of vetch (a perennial ground cover with pea-shaped golden yellow flowers), Barbara and her husband built a deck that overlooks the Gore Range to one side and the rounded peak of Old Baldy to the other. The rushing waters of Gore Creek flow below the wood structure, and the White River National Forest stretches beyond. "This is where I get inspiration for my gardens," says Barbara. "I try to mix plants as haphazardly as they would occur in nature, without introducing color combinations that clash."

Like other addicted mountain gardeners, Barbara's enthusiasm and expertise extend beyond her own gardens. She is a board member of the Vail Alpine Garden Foundation and an active volunteer with the foundation's sponsored projects and developments, like the Vail Festival of Flowers and the Betty Ford Alpine Gardens. "Our mission is two-fold," she says. "We want Vail to be known as much for its flowers as its skiing, and we want to show gardeners in mountain communities what grows effectively at high altitude."

Established in 1987, the Betty Ford Alpine Gardens, with four different garden areas, are named after the former First Lady for her many contributions to the Vail area. At an altitude of 8,200 feet, they are the highest public gardens in North America and among the highest in the world. There is an Alpine Display Garden featuring a variety of alpine and subalpine plants; a Mountain Perennial Garden with traditional and unusual perennials, trees and shrubs; a Mountain Meditation Garden; and an Alpine Rock Garden displaying an extensive collection of alpine plants from North America and mountainous regions around the world.

During June and July, with flower-filled baskets hanging from every lamp post in the town of Vail, the Vail Festival of Flowers sponsors an annual garden contest. Area homeowners enter their gardens for judging, and prizes are awarded in a variety of categories. Barbara's favorite volunteer activity is bicycling to award-winning gardens and planting honorary markers on the designated lawns.

"I feel so lucky," she says. "I love working in the Betty Ford Gardens and promoting the efforts of mountain gardeners. As for my own gardens, I lose myself. Sometimes I'll look up from weeding or pruning and realize it's nighttime and I'm working in the dark."

Vail is lucky, too. Energetic, visionary, and generous, Barbara is the kind of Garden Lady many a mountain town would like to claim.

CANDY TUFT, SNOW-IN-SUMMER, PERENNIAL BACHELOR BUTTON, AND LUPINE

Lamb's ear, lady's mantle, and yellow archangel

Barbara Walker and Chip Shevlin

Steamboat Springs

When Barbara Walker and Chip Shevlin moved to Steamboat Springs from New Jersey, they decided to start their first garden. A New England cottage garden pictured in a magazine seemed like a fine model for developing their own garden plan. "It worked," says Barbara as she displays the glossy, yellowing pages stored in a drawer ever since. "We adapted the symmetry and design of that garden to our own space, and substituted plants that thrive in the west for moisture-loving eastern varieties."

Their Victorian home is now surrounded by Barbara and Chip's creations, gardens that are breathtaking. Honeysuckle, silver lace, and trumpet vines climb along fences and trellises, forming a lush backdrop for plantings full of color and foliar interest. On the shady side of the house, the grays and silvers of 'Beacon Silver' lamium and snow-in-summer glisten among clear yellow primroses and violet alpine asters under the arching branches of a 'Bridal Veil' spirea shrub. The pastel flowers of blue mist spirea, lilac, and 'Sunburst' hypericum shrubs float over mounds of dragon's blood sedums, creeping phlox, and potentilla in a sunny corner.

Shrubs are important to Barbara and Chip's garden design. 'Annabelle' hydrangeas, with large leaves and ball-sized clusters of creamy white flowers; 'Allegheny' viburnums, with dark green leaves and light yellow flowers followed by red berries; and burning bush, renowned for its brilliant scarlet foliage in the fall, are some of the shrubs that add texture, structure, and seasonal interest to the garden. Barbara likes to plant different varieties of the same species together, like alpine and 'Red Lake' currant shrubs. The same-shaped but different-sized leaves of the shrubs provide a subtle and effective contrast.

Hanging pots filled with gazanias, sweet William, lobelia, English ivy, and the cascading golden buttons of moneywort reflect Barbara's gift for creating layers of texture and color. Articulate as well as talented, she has many useful gardening tips. "Create a story in the garden," she says. "Build a rich setting for a specific plant species so that it shines on its own yet complements everything around it. Think about blooming times, and please—plant things that prove the experts wrong."

Steamboat Springs

In two summers, Kendall and Chapman Geer transformed a bare lot into a garden paradise. This is no easy feat when your soil is filled with rocks, your growing season is very short, and your winters give new meaning to the word "freeze."

Set in the wide Yampa Valley, Steamboat Springs is a relaxed mountain community surrounded by cattle ranches and renowned for its world-class skiing. The Geers' property backs onto a golf course and overlooks the ski area. The home itself is perched at the top of a steep incline. The Geers have added rocks and boulders to the front slope to create an ideal environment for growing plants. "The slope provides protection from winds and harsh weather, and the rocks hold heat, creating a microclimate where plants will thrive," says Kendall, who has attended master gardening classes. "The flowers in our yard bloom much longer than they would out in the open."

Irises, peonies, delphiniums, gayfeathers, and yarrow join in a pleasing mix of color and texture along the hillside. Potentilla, sandcherry, and barberry shrubs provide structure. One of the Geers' best garden performers, 'Miss Kim' lilac shrubs, complement the front yard perennials and extend into a border of wildflowers at the side of the house. Poppies, columbines, bachelor buttons, and sweet rockets stream through aspen trees and more boulders and rocks. Metal dinosaur-like sculptures that Chapman created peer through the trees.

In the backyard, Chapman dug a 100-foot-long trough for a stream. Water is pumped over tiers of flat rocks at one end of the yard and cascades in a waterfall to fill the stream bed below. The stream flows across the length of the yard to a water lily pond surrounded by serviceberry shrubs, wild roses,

and ornamental grasses. "I looked at natural streams long and hard before designing my own water feature," says Chapman. "It's not that hard to do, and not that expensive. I used rubber liners with old carpet underneath for the stream bed."

Chapman also installed a series of lights at the base of the aspen trees that surround the yard. The lights illuminate the white bark of the trees at night,

creating a perfect backdrop for the summer parties the Geers host for family and friends. "Chapman's thinking 'Hollywood' when he's working in the garden," says Kendall. "I'm just trying to make plants blend together in a natural setting." Luckily for Steamboat party-goers and plant-lovers alike, the Geers' different approaches combine in a garden tour de force.

Vi Lake and Stormy Werking
Glenwood Springs

Gardens evolve for many different reasons—the desire to create, to nurture, to commune with nature. Stormy Werking's garden grew out of her love for her mother.

Stormy remembers the day she received the call that her mother, Vi Lake, had suffered a heart attack. Rushing to the hospital, she had no idea what condition her mother would be in. Luckily, Vi recovered and was soon able to return home.

Vi has lived in her small home among sprawling gardens of roses, ferns, and violets in the west end of Glenwood Canyon since 1962. The house and garden are in a spot she loves, shady, secluded, and tucked in a hollow between the canyon walls with No Name Creek gurgling behind. After Vi's heart attack, Stormy and husband Scott wanted her to move closer to them. Vi refused. So Stormy and Scott did the next best thing—they built a house next to Vi's instead. They also improved the driveway snaking down to the houses from the main road and installed a leach field on the other side of the drive.

Then Stormy got the gardening bug. At first she only wanted to replace her mother's garden areas destroyed by construction and to create some pretty places for Vi to look at as she recuperated, but soon everywhere Stormy looked she saw an ideal place for flowers. With help from Scott, she converted the leech field into a huge circular garden with sandstone paths and flagstones winding through masses of cosmos, yarrow, hollyhocks, sunflowers, phlox, larkspurs, irises, and more. Boulders dug up during construction now stand among the colorful array of blooms. Sweet peas climb over the gate to the area that is ringed by scrub oaks.

The barren strip by the driveway was the next garden project. As with the leach field, Stormy and

Scott brought in yards of topsoil and peat moss to amend the rocky clay soil. Stormy then tucked anemones, violas, and primroses into and around rock walls and planted a mixture of pincushion flowers, asters, gaillardia, and Iceland poppies behind them.

Wildflowers line the drive down to the two homes where more gardens explode with color and interest. Purple clematis and pink climbing roses wind up lattices attached to Vi's clapboard house. Blue spruce bordering the front yard and a weeping

willow tree in the center shade the garden in front of the house. Columbines, lamium, and violas are just some of the plants that thrive in the shady beds. Surrounding stone bird baths, lanterns, and benches are plantain lilies, hostas, and bleeding hearts while annuals like forget-me-nots and bicolored butterfly flowers have reseeded everywhere.

Through a trellis arch covered with roses, a path leads from Vi's house to Stormy and Scott's. The Werkings' equally shady yard is lined with bright pink impatiens that Stormy intends to "buy by the truckload" next year because of their fresh, bright color that lasts all summer long.

Vi's favorite garden—her rose garden—sits behind her house, where rows of lavender, pink, red, white, and fuchsia hybrid roses line the banks of No Name Creek. Vi loves to sit by the creek and breathe in the fragrance from the roses while she watches birds fly overhead and perch in the cedars and junipers by the creek. As she watches the creek flow by, Vi reminisces about her deep roots in the Glenwood Springs area. In the early 1800s, Vi's grandfather moved his family to New Castle, a town west of Glenwood Springs where coal mines were operational through the early 1900s. Three sons died in a mine explosion that killed forty-nine miners in 1896. Vi's grandfather became Glenwood Springs' first night marshal. Her father was a Glenwood Springs policeman, and Vi followed the family tradition by working for the city's police department and then the sheriff's office.

Vi has softer memories, too. She remembers her mother's garden filled with asters, cosmos, and roses. "It looked a lot like Stormy's does now," she says. Her grandmother was a gardener as well, and Vi can still picture the bleeding hearts, irises, daisies, and lilacs that grew in her garden by the Roaring Fork River.

"Gardening runs in the family," says Vi. "After all, my full name is Viola."

Glenwood Springs

Flying home to Nebraska after World War II, Ed Niemann talked over plans for civilian life with his fellow pilot and best friend. Perhaps as an antidote to their war experiences, the two men decided they would go into "growing things." Ed's friend ended up a banker, but Ed remained true to his dream. After years of apprenticeship in a greenhouse, Ed moved to Glenwood Springs in 1952 with his wife, Naomi, and started his own nursery, Glenwood Gardens, with just five-hundred dollars. It was a gutsy move. When Naomi's mother, used to gardening in black Nebraska loam, visited Naomi and Ed for the first time, she was incredulous. "She asked how anything would ever grow in this clay and rock," says Naomi.

The couple were not discouraged. They set up shop in a conservatory-style greenhouse with historical ties to the region. The structure was moved from its original location by the Crystal River in Redstone, thirty miles south, where it had been the property of John C. Osgood, an eccentric coal magnate. Osgood attempted to establish an ideal community of beauty and culture for workers and management alike during Redstone's short-lived boom years at the turn of the century. The greenhouse, resembling a giant glass honeycomb, is still an area landmark, visible from Interstate 70.

Ed and Naomi's business thrived through hard work, long hours, and love. The closest greenhouse to Aspen for many years, Glenwood Gardens provided plants, expertise, and services for residents within a fifty-mile radius of Glenwood Springs. Perhaps their most famous client was Eleanor Roosevelt, who made an order while visiting her son at his ranch in Meeker, north of Rifle. Many early Aspenites, like Walter Paepcke, one of the town's first benefactors, and author Leon Uris, placed regular orders. For forty years, the Neimanns' business kept pace with the growing popularity and changing character of the region.

"We married people and we buried them," says Naomi, referring to the many flowers they supplied

over the years for area residents. "We loved this business. It was our life. We cried when we sold it and drove away for the last time."

Now retired to a hillside home on the outskirts of Glenwood Springs, the Niemanns are actively engaged in creating a garden that reflects their horticultural knowledge and Naomi's love of summer-long color and bloom. Overlooking Mount Sopris with Glenwood Canyon below, the garden's borders are filled with bright perennials and annuals that not only withstand the tough hillside conditions and clay soil, but seem gaily lined up to enjoy the view. Among larkspur, flax, and pink snapdragons, a stolid sunflower that sprouted from seed dropped by a bird peers over the crowd of blooms. Rudbeckias, balloon flowers, and delphinium are more perennials that thrive in the windblown borders. In protected beds along the side of the house are pink and red roses with purple pansies growing underneath. Naomi points out her many favorite roses: 'Betty Prior,' the single petal floribunda; 'Queen Elizabeth,' a hardy grandiflora rose; and the hybrid tea, 'Tropicana.' At one edge of the Neimanns' property, purple clematis and pink morning glory vines intertwine across cattle fences.

Among the annuals that Naomi depends on for long-lasting bloom, the satiny pink, white, and red godetias are her favorites. They not only appear in her borders but in containers, like the pot that Naomi's grandmother made soap in. Naomi also loves petunias and geraniums—especially the varieties introduced by plant breeder, Charlie Weddle. She remembers Weddle, who had greenhouses in Paonia and Grand Junction, for the ruffled, doubled form and vibrant color of the plants he hybridized. Naomi also recommends bidens, willowy plants topped by tiny, yellow flowers that bloom continuously wherever she puts them.

Like many avid gardeners, Naomi can't keep to her property boundaries. As the garden drops down the hill into her neighbors' domain, Naomi throws out seeds and peach and apricot pits so that anyone traveling up the hill will eventually have something beautiful to look at. Oxeye daisies, chicory, and wild lilac sprawl over the area for now. In years to come, Naomi will have left a legacy of beauty she can only imagine—and her mother would not believe.

Basalt

Lynn Nichols thinks that neurotic project-lovers make the best gardeners. She blames her own "project gene" on her father, a Kansas City businessman who encouraged these tendencies throughout her child-hood. "We spent summers in Basalt," she says, "and now I'm living—and gardening—where my happiest childhood memories took place."

Lynn and her family live on the Cap-K Ranch, a farming and cattle operation situated along the Frying Pan River east of Basalt. The ranch spreads through a broad valley with red cliffs to one side and the sparkling river, renowned for its fishing, to the other. The ranch is named in honor of Lynn's mother and aunt who endured harsh conditions to transform the land into a working ranch. Childhood summers at the ranch were idyllic, and Lynn is happily shaping a life in these beloved surroundings that includes raising a family, running the day-to-day operations of the ranch (as co-owner with her three sisters), working as a landscape architect, and gardening.

One of Lynn and her husband's first projects was to renovate a clapboard house on the property into their home. When they began work, they found that the white siding covered an old log house built 100 years before. Excited, they disassembled the entire house, carefully marking each section and rebuilding piece by piece. Although they built additions, it is hard to tell where the old house ends and the new one begins. Once the house was completed, Lynn looked to the yard, creating the gardens that had been brewing in her project-hungry mind.

Luckily, Lynn loves the physical labor involved in gardening. Finding that the silty ranch soil near the house was compacted with clumps of clay running through it, Lynn excavated an eight-foot pit where she wanted the gardens and filled it with loamy topsoil. Next to the house she planted aspen trees and created beds for a winding shade garden. With water from a pump, she created a brook that circles the central, sunny garden area and added paths that amble through it.

Planting flowers was Lynn's next project. Using perennials native or adapted to her region, Lynn created artful gardens of plants placed carefully to best dramatize different combinations of color, shape, and size. Lynn especially likes the effect of combining "wilder, looser plants" like feathery meadow rue with the "stiff, architectural" varieties such as the erect thistle-like sea holly. Combining plants with contrasting foliage—like glossy, dark green holly with frilly, lime-colored ferns—is another way Lynn creates interest and texture in her gardens. She points to a grouping of blue delphinium, yellow St. John's wort, and white liatris that creates a combi-nation of crisp, bright colors she especially likes.

Columbines, astilbes, hosta, lady's mantle, wild ginger, and thyme grow under the shade of aspen trees at the side of the house. In the central, sunny

bed, waves of delphiniums, lupines, penstemons, Asiatic lilies, mallows, and gentians form a yard-size bouquet of colorful blooms. To keep track of her ever-changing garden, Lynn keeps index cards of all her plants sorted by color and months of bloom. She also takes weekly photographs of her gardens to plan for the next season during the long winter months. "I love the fact that next summer the garden will be completely different," she says.

Behind the house, cherry trees border a series of raised beds filled with lettuce, radishes, carrots, daisies, and sunflowers. Cows graze in the background while plump guinea fowl waddle across the back patio and through the beds, pecking at the ground. The little "vacuum cleaners" keep Lynn's gardens free of aphids, earwigs, and grasshoppers.

Rounding the corner to the other side of the house, a free-form wildflower garden of daisies, poppies, Queen Anne's lace, phlox, fireweed, and sunflowers spreads through an orchard of apple, apricot, and cherry trees. Although it is a carefree type of garden for a project-oriented type of gardener ("I throw seeds out in the spring and mow it in the fall"), Lynn thinks this might be her favorite garden area.

"Every Mother's Day we invite neighborhood families here. The kids run through the wildflowers and pick whatever they want," says Lynn.

Childhood memories just keep growing at Cap-K Ranch.

Basalt

"Forget Giverny," is Angela Foster's advice to Colorado gardeners. She refers to painter Claude Monet's gardens, located northeast of Paris in the lush Seine River Valley. And she is not criticizing the breathtaking tapestry of color and shape that Monet created in his gardens and captured on canvas. She is urging Colorado gardeners to shape their own garden aesthetic based on the plants and growing conditions of their region. Instead of trying to copy Monet's lovely sweep of pink tulips and blue forget-me-nots, she suggests planting vincas among bleeding hearts. The pink drops of bleeding heart blooms nodding over the tiny blue flowers of the creeping vincas will give the same effect. "Honor where you are," says Angela. "Take your message from the natural world you live in."

A transplant from Great Britain, Angela has lived in the Roaring Fork River Valley since the 1970s. She is a gardening columnist for *The Aspen Times*, and a passionate and knowledgeable gardener. Her gardens in Basalt surround the 100-year-old farmhouse where she and her family live. Instead of expanding the farmhouse to accommodate their family's needs, the Fosters "honored" the place that they came to. They restored the rustic log building to its original state and scale, and spread their living quarters among the other farm structures nearby. The arrangement created a challenge in designing a garden that would be seen from many different vantage points. As is so often the case with gardening, the design challenge turned into a blessing. The resulting garden is set among the fruit trees of the farm's orchard, incorporates existing plantings like dark red rambler roses that grow around the farmhouse, and has perfect dimension, shape, and form.

In the spring Angela's garden brims with the colors of the alpine meadows that provide her gardening inspiration. Some of her favorite combinations are the magenta, cream, and pink owl clover

blooming alongside blue penstemon, red paintbrush, yellow balsam, and white and soft blue columbine— flowers she has found while hiking in the Elk Mountain Range. In mid to late summer, Angela likes brightly colored flowers that reflect the hot, harsh weather conditions. Towering electric blue delphinium, red Maltese cross, black-eyed Susans, and foxgloves swim in an eddy of yellow and orange daylilies, spikes of purple veronica, fuchsia phlox, and white daisies. It is a vision worthy of a frame and place of honor in a gallery.

Angela readily admits that her garden is where she "paints." And although she admires Monet, it is the bold, jarring colors and contrasting patterns of Matisse that drive her own aesthetic. "I like creating wiggly lines of vibrant color throughout my garden," says Angela. Although her garden is a result of observation, careful study, and planning, creating a sense of being "almost out of control" is another important element in Angela's garden concept. "After all, nature is in control," she says.

Calling her garden an "English cottage garden with alpine meadow colors," Angela encourages other gardeners to experiment with the cottage garden tradition. Writing in her column for *The Aspen Times*, she refers to the origins of the cottage garden —a tradition born of the hardship and poverty of peasants' wives who sprinkled flowers into the small vegetable plots in front of their homes. Heartened by the bit of beauty introduced into their lives, the women began to trade plants with each other until their gardens grew into the "colorful blowsiness" that we have come to love. With "humour and patience, and an ability to accept failure and to accept being humbled by the elements," Angela promises that Roaring Fork gardeners and beyond can create gardens of color and texture reflecting the natural beauty of their own singular piece of earth.

Laurie McBride

Old Snowmass

Laurie McBride's garden in Old Snowmass is the kind of place where you could imagine a foreign movie being filmed—something romantic, surprising, out of this world. Set in the bright, clear sun at 8,000 feet, her garden boasts views of Mount Sopris and the sweep of the Elk Mountains in the background. Daisies race across the acre-size garden where flower beds, wrought iron tables and chairs, scarecrows, sculptures, arbors, bridges, English bedsteads, fences from Paris, statues, and urns are placed at leisurely intervals. "I like profusion, whimsy, and the south of France," says Laurie as she describes the area. "It was a garden that just happened."

The garden surrounds the McBrides' stucco home and looks out on the fields of their Lost Marbles Ranch, a cattle operation. Many different areas make up Laurie's garden tapestry, each with its own distinct character and charm. Some areas are intimate, dedicated to friends and family members. For her mother, Laurie planted daisies, allium, columbines, and violas in a spot shaded by aspen trees. A gilded marker sits in the profusion of blooms and pays tribute to her mother's musical gifts. A quote from Maumonier reads: "There is always music amongst the trees in the garden, but our hearts must be very quiet to hear it."

The brick patio at the rear of the house resembles a country market where carved chairs and tables are surrounded by terra-cotta pots brimming with alyssum, lobelia, and violas. An English bed frame sits in the middle of the English Garden where lilacs, delphinium, roses, and irises jostle for space. Part of a fence discovered from an old home in Aspen swings open as a gate to one of the more dramatic garden spots. A few steps away, you can look through a series of arbors, across a bridge spanning a brook, and past a sea of daisies to a statue of Saint Francis of Assisi framed by the mountains beyond. All the arbors, bridges, and trellises were fashioned from twigs and branches by Laurie's father. Their rustic beauty and simplicity provide a pleasing and unifying garden theme.

Humor is definitely another repeating element in Laurie's garden. Lolling by the statue of Saint Francis is a scarecrow sporting a blue jean dress and pearls with a pot of pink petunias on her head. A sculpture garden of bronze animals crafted by Laurie's sister-in-law sprawls nearby. A frog with its arms folded behind its head, legs stretched out, and a happy grin was made in honor of Laurie herself. Croquet wickets serve as plant tag holders. One of the wickets by the plant known as *saponaria* (or soapwort) sports a tag that reads "sopapilla." It's not a misprint. "Some day I'm going to have a party and misname everything," says Laurie referring to her frustration with the Latin names for plants.

Creating a garden of interest and character is one thing, but getting anything to grow at 8,000 feet is a more basic—and critical—concern. Laurie says it is well worth the effort to learn high altitude gardening techniques. The cooler air and sharp drop in temperatures in the morning and at night result in flowers that bloom with vibrant, crisp colors that can't be duplicated anywhere else. Like the other gardeners in her growing region, Laurie raves about how well certain plants do in the mountains. Her sturdy delphiniums and pincushion flowers grow to five feet tall. Daylilies, yarrow, peonies, lupine, and campanula are other plants that do well for her. The old roses that she gets from High Country Rosarium in Denver are also good performers at her altitude.

Laurie's best gardening tip is to "trick things into growing" by creating microclimates and sheltered areas in the garden. "My lavender thinks it's growing in Zone 5 instead of Zone 3 because I tucked it around some stones," she says. "I planted Maltese cross against the shelter of the house and it spread everywhere."

The manure tea Laurie makes from her llama Inca's droppings (dubbed "Inca's gold" by the McBrides) may be still another secret to Laurie's gardening success. In the end, however, Laurie delights in her garden as a "reminder of the cycle of life." Looking across her garden of vegetables, flowers, trees, and found objects, she asks, "Isn't it thrilling to see things grow?"

Katherine Ware

Carbondale

Encircling her home in Carbondale, K. (short for Katherine) Ware's garden is a one-woman spectacular that defies the harsh weather conditions and stiff, clay soil of her growing area. Neighbors in her subdivision of new homes are still amazed—and inspired—by the oasis of flowers, trees, and shrubs that she has coaxed and hounded into existence.

A pioneering attitude has always come easily to K. She lived all over the Roaring Fork and Crystal River Valleys before settling in Carbondale. She describes herself as one of the wave of "hippies" to arrive in Carbondale in the 1970s when it was a sleepy cattle town. With others, she helped found Carbondale's first public radio station and the Mountain Fair, a popular regional event.

Like most towns around it, Carbondale has breathtaking natural beauty and an interesting history. Ringed by mountains and forests, the town sits at the confluence of the Crystal and Roaring Fork Rivers. Carbondale was founded in the late 1800s by two merchants who were waylaid near the town by a band of Ute Indians. The new community thrived— first as the site of the area's Denver & Rio Grande train station, and then as a potato-growing town. Not only did the renowned 'McClure' and 'Perfect Peachblow' potatoes originate in Carbondale, the town produced the author of the definitive book, *The Potato*. Unfortunately, the unrelenting planting of potatoes over many years left the soil depleted, and the potato industry died out.

K. and her husband moved to a former potato farm outside of Carbondale to raise their family, and it was there that K. started her first garden. After years of laying fallow, the soil around her house returned to the rich, black loam ideal for growing potatoes. In her "perfect growing environment," K. grew corn, beans, broccoli, and "tons of flowers."

Moving to the subdivision in town was a shock for K. Although located in a beautiful area on the edge of Carbondale with the Crystal River running behind the house and a view of the sandstone

formation called Red Hill, K.'s new home stood shoulder to shoulder with other neighbors' on soil "that was nothing but rock." Missing her old environment of wide open spaces and lush gardens, K. got to work. She flagged down trucks that were hauling away soil from newly excavated home sites and designated her own yard as the new dumping ground. Twenty-five truckloads of soil and countless bags of straw and manure later, K. found herself standing in "mountains of dirt." As neighbors gaped from their flat and treeless front lawns, she spent a summer creating berms of soil that surrounded the front yard and churned the backyard into an area of rich soil reminiscent of her former potato farm garden.

The following summer, K. planted the front berms with the old-fashioned and hardy flowers she loves—hollyhocks, artemisia, veronica, wild roses, clover, and Queen Anne's lace—among a forest of trees and shrubs. Lines of red-twig dogwood, spruce, buckthorn, currant, cranberry, and burning bushes wind through the berms like the spirals of a pinwheel to the sunken patio area in the middle. Here, hidden from the world, is where K. spreads out in a lawn chair, sips tea, reads books, and savors the beauty around her. "I'm glad the garden is in the front where people can see it," says K. "I just don't want anyone to know I'm here in my fortress."

In the backyard, Canadian red cherry trees and an Amur maple shade the deck. K. loves the deep red color of the maple's leaves in the fall. Sunflowers stand at attention at the back fence, saluting Red Hill across the neighboring fields.

Since K.'s chutzpah has resulted in a Garden of Eden in the improbable clay soil of Carbondale, lawns up and down her street are filling with trees, shrubs, flowers, and hills. But K.'s influence spread further, beyond age and city limits. Director of the Mini College, a preschool in Glenwood Springs, K. whiles away the long winter months by directing her preschoolers in the fine arts of planting seeds and nurturing seedlings on the classroom windowsills. This new wave of gardeners is learning planting tips and the love of gardening from "the pro," ensuring a new generation of gardeners.

Redstone

In 1984, Peter and Ann Martin took a chance and fell in love. Although they had decided to move to Santa Fe, a friend urged them to "just take a look at Carbondale." They drove to the town and then kept going, turning southwest along Highway 133 through the Crystal River Valley. Smitten with the beauty of the lush valley with the sparkling river to one side, red cliff walls to the other, and Mount Sopris looming ahead, Peter and Ann ended their drive in the historic coal mining town of Redstone where their love affair was complete. No one who knows the area could blame them. Today they are still very much in love—with their home near the historic Redstone Inn, the spectacular countryside that surrounds them, and the unique beauty of their gardens that area growing conditions have helped to shape.

Redstone was founded in 1899 by John C. Osgood, who operated a lucrative coal mining claim in the area and started the Colorado Fuel & Iron Company. Lines of coke ovens still squat across the road from the town. Osgood's short-lived empire brought the likes of John C. Rockefeller and J. P. Morgan to dine at his Redstone Tudor manor, which he called "Cleveholm." Envisioning an ideal community, Osgood built an inn and dining hall for bachelor miners and a village of multicolored Swiss chalets for miners with families. Where the town's schoolhouse once stood is now the site of the Martin home— "a discreet 100 yards away from the manor house," says Peter.

The Martin home is surrounded by sweeping, manicured lawns. Aspens are scattered through the area close to the home and through the many graceful, curved flower beds. The backyard features a large red rock echoing the color of the surrounding cliffs. The cultivated areas drift into the forest beyond where firs and pines form a lush green backdrop. Peter likes taking his grandchildren to an enormous 250-year-old ponderosa pine where the kids can see how small they are in the scheme of things. Chickadees, pine

siskins, and three kinds of grosbeak are only some of the species that frequent the wilder gardens near the forested areas. The entire yard is filled with bird song.

Originally from Kansas, the Martins have adapted enthusiastically to the gardening challenges of the Redstone area. They enjoy gardening together (Ann prunes and Peter "experiments") and the creative outlet it affords them. Extremes of weather are their number one complaint. "Spring in the Rockies begins on the fourth of July here," jokes Ann. "We don't dare plant annuals until after the first of June."

Peter is especially grateful for the long-lasting color of the pansies that line many of the flower beds. He takes issue with people who call someone wimpy a pansy. "Pansies are tough," he says. He waxes more eloquently over the Siberian irises whose blossoms "float like butterflies" above their stalks. Lupines, delphiniums, columbines, hostas, and daisies are other perennials that do well at this 7,200-foot altitude. Peter has tried to push his plant envelope by introducing perennials from warmer climates into his garden. The fern-leafed peony with its dark crimson flowers and lacy foliage is one of his most successful experiments. Although roses only grow as annuals in the Martin's yard, Asiatic lilies thrive in garden borders. One of Peter and Ann's favorite garden areas is by the back deck where fifteen different types of columbine crowd together in a mass of yellow, red, blue, purple, and pure white blooms "as big as your hand." Peter also loves the ten-foot-tall cranberry viburnum bush that produces huge white blooms in summer and is "glorious with bright red berries" in the fall.

Flower-hungry deer are the Martins' second greatest gardening complaint and they have come up with a unique solution for deterring them. Every night, Ann and Peter lay lightweight, porous row covers over their flower beds, and every morning they remove them to reveal pristine, untouched blooms. The process is time-consuming, but the Martins seem to enjoy this part of their joint gardening ritual as much as the more mundane chores of weeding, pruning, and deadheading. Surrounded by their gardens filled with blooms and birdsong, the Martins seem to be the perfect couple who have made a truly perfect match.

Redstone

Bonnie and Clark Cretti live across the street—and in a gardening sense, worlds apart—from Ann and Peter Martin. While the Martins' property sits in the open with mountain vistas and forest spreading out below the slope of their backyard, the Crettis' property is tucked into a hill and shaded by groves of mature aspen trees extending into their yard from the forest directly behind them. Probably because of cold air trapped longer in their protected area, the Crettis' growing season is three weeks behind their neighbors' living a one-minute walk away. "I'm jealous of Peter and Ann in May, but they're jealous of us later on," says Clark.

Indeed, while the Martins are constantly digging up rocks that push through their garden soil, Clark and Bonnie enjoy the advantage of rich, black humus from the ancient forest decaying beneath them. They also enjoy a thatch of soft native grass that stays weed-free and never needs mowing.

The Crettis' home is in the historic Redstone Firehouse amidst a sprawl of perennials, wildflowers, and grasses that climb the hill to the side of the house and extend naturally into the surrounding forest. Clark discovered Redstone as a young man and, for over twenty-five years, has found reason after reason to stay. For a time he was the caretaker for the firehouse. It was owned by an "elderly gentleman" who liked the deep shade created by the groves of aspen growing like weeds in the side yard. Clark envisioned a more meadow-like setting, but he loved the building with its original weather vane sitting on the roof, its huge double windows that had served as portals for the fire engines, the moss on the patio, and the old stone wall that stood in front as it had since Redstone's pioneer days.

When the firehouse went up for sale, Clark purchased it, knowing the old building and its grounds had been waiting for him. He restored the crumbling brick work, painted doors and trim, and built brick additions. When one of the aspens fell over in the side yard during a storm, Clark felt he was given

permission to clear more of the "weedy" aspens from the grounds and create a sunnier space for a garden.

Clark and Bonnie have their own separate garden areas. Clark enjoys the wild, uncultivated look of "his" gardens closer to the house. Towering delphiniums on sturdy stalks and three-foot yellow columbines line the stone wall in front. In the side yard, deep pink lupines mix with irises among wild snapdragons, sweet William, coral bells, painted daisies, larkspur, and mounds of sweet woodruff. Surrounding a stone birdbath are violas, columbines, snow-in-summer, and sedums. Thanks to the lingering, cool air, Clark claims that tulips and daffodils planted in this area keep their crisp, bright color well into summer. Bonnie is equally enthusiastic about "her" wild garden of vegetables and flowers closer to the woods. Inspired by the book, *The Secret Garden*, Bonnie has created a pleasing jumble of daisies, sweet peas, onions, lettuce, raspberries, strawberries, columbines, lupines, and Maltese cross that resembles an English cottage garden. Hummingbirds motor happily through all the garden areas.

While Peter Martin claims that Clark is the more compulsive gardener ("He's out there shoveling snow banks off the front retaining wall in April!" says Peter), Clark points out that nothing could be more compulsive than Peter's ritual covering of flower beds to deter deer. Clark claims an easier solution to the deer problem. He places sprinkler heads connected to motion detectors at strategic points around the yard. When the deer approach, they trigger the motion detector and a water jet that frightens off the animals. The beauty of this solution is the lack of unsightly apparatus—netting, tin cans, and the like—and the fact that the water spray is harmless.

"And about the shoveling," says Clark. "I find huge columbines blooming inside those snow drifts in April!"

Bonnie reveals that Clark's gardening skills and ingenuity are inherited. "His grandfather was a peach grower," says Bonnie, "and everyone in his family is a gardening fanatic. There's a drill when they visit each other's gardens. No matter what, they always say, 'It never looked better!'"

And in the case of the Cretti's wild, secret, and enchanted gardens, it's probably true.

Crested Butte

The drive north from Gunnison to the Easley-Sherwood home, just outside Crested Butte, is through rolling ranchland with the chiseled peaks of Mount Crested Butte in the distance. Meadows packed with wildflowers stretch along either side of the highway. The vibrant colors of scarlet gilias, lupines, and alpine sunflowers glisten in the crisp, thin air at 9,300 feet in altitude.

Residents of Crested Butte since 1970, Marnie Easley and Woody Sherwood value the pristine beauty of their town and its surroundings. As owners of Rocky Mountain Trees and Landscaping, they are adamant about honoring and protecting their environment. Marnie urges area gardeners to learn to cohabitate with the area's wild animals. "They were here first," says Marnie. "Rabbits decimated my crab apple trees, but I still love watching them. I decided my garden didn't need to be perfect."

The Easley-Sherwood log home is set in an aspen grove with Gunnison National Forest behind it. Under the aspen canopy, native shrubs, grasses, and plants flow from the wilderness area onto the property and mix with Indian paintbrush, sulfur flowers, gilias, and fescue grasses grown from seed. The home's back deck overlooks an open meadow where blue flax spreads among lilacs and wild roses, and deep purple clematis winds along the branches of serviceberry shrubs.

Perennial beds circle the house. To survive the long, cold winters of the region, these plants must be tough. The four to five feet of annual snow acts as a heavy mulch, either crushing or protecting the growth underneath. Like florists' bouquets kept fresh in a freezer, the perennials that do emerge from Crested Butte's heavy snow have intensely bright colors and long, albeit late, season blooms. In June, bleeding hearts, tulips, and daffodils fill the Easley-Sherwoods' perennial beds. Oriental poppies, Siberian irises, lupines, penstemons, and columbines reach their peak in July. August sees a procession of rudbeckias, sunflowers, monkshood, and bee balm.

As persevering as the plants they grow, the Easley-Sherwoods continually introduce new plants into their region —like yellow monkeyflowers, cranesbill geraniums, and Canadian roses. "We love the challenge," says Marnie. "It's fun to see what grows."

Rosie Catmur

Crested Butte

Although she grew up in England, surrounded by her father's gardens of lilies, peonies, and roses, Rosie Catmur never thought of gardening herself until she moved to Crested Butte.

Rosie and her husband, Martin, moved to Crested Butte from Denver to find a simpler, more meaningful life in the laid-back mountain community. They bought a bed-and-breakfast and set down roots with their two children.

Along the front of the Catmurs' Cristiana Guesthaus, Rosie transformed a gravel parking strip into wide berms filled with colorful perennials. "This was a bare and sad spot when we first came here," Rosie says. "I nearly broke my wrist trying to dig through the rocks. Finally, I just added topsoil and peat on top of the whole mess. After a few years, the garden took off."

Rosie's favorite garden area is a haze of pink and blue that she catches sight of whenever she rounds the corner to the guest house. Jacob's ladders, dianthus, columbines, and painted daisies wind through boulders and rocks covered with creeping thymes and sedums. Farther on, spikes of blue catmint mingle with white larkspurs, blue pincushion flowers, and bright red poppies among small firs. Snow-in-summer, oxeye chamomiles, and butter and eggs (erect perennials that bear yellow snapdragon-like flowers) run rampant through the plantings. Rosie lovingly calls the invasive plants her "weeds."

Native plants and wildflowers that Rosie encounters on hikes are also in her garden. She relies on her friend, nursery owner Marnie Easley, for native hybrids that thrive in cultivated garden spaces. White bellflowers, mountain bluebells, dwarf sunflowers, and the bluish-white pasqueflowers seem right at home in Rosie's rambling, natural landscape. The star-shaped edelweiss, a plant that grows in European mountains, makes a bright appearance in the garden's borders as well.

Rosie's passion for flowers is not restricted to her own garden. Every July, Rosie joins with friends and fellow gardeners to coordinate the Crested Butte Wildflower Festival. The week-long event offers classes, hikes, and programs and celebrates Crested Butte's 1989 designation as the Wildflower Capitol of Colorado.

"We love to share this amazing beauty," Rosie says.

Crested Butte

A fence inspired Maura Bailey's first garden. Along with most other fences in Crested Butte, the fence that stood between her restaurant, Le Soupçon, and her neighbor's home collapsed every winter under the four feet of heavy snow that blanketed the town. The neighbor, who wanted a barrier to protect her property from restaurant traffic, was frustrated. "I decided to make a berm for planting flowers where we kept building fences," says Maura. "Now a garden stands between me and my neighbor. We learned that gardens foster better friendships than fences any day."

Located in a side alley off one of the main streets in town, Maura's garden is well-loved by locals and attracts admiring exclamations from passersby. Across waves of wildflowers, herbs, and perennials that mingle in a riot of bright colors, Victorian buildings in shades of pink, yellow, and blue appear against the white-streaked peaks of Crested Butte and Mount Gothic. Fireweed, a tall wildflower with spires of rose-purple blooms, leads the parade, followed by pink and red poppies, yellow lilies, pink yarrow, and deep blue veronicas. A ribbon of white Shasta daisies weaves through the plantings. Pink garlic chives and clumps of comfrey that Maura uses in her restaurant nestle with wild violets at the base of the taller plants.

The tiny 1916-vintage log cabin housing Le Soupçon faces the long berm of flowers. At the cabin's lace-curtained windows, pansies, violets, and marigolds spill from window boxes. To the side of the restaurant, cool weather herbs like French tarragon, chives, mint, oregano, and marjoram grow among violets and columbines in raised beds. Maura says columbines love Crested Butte's cool weather and reseed all over her gardens.

Looking at her fence of flowers, Maura admits the garden is on her neighbor's property, not her own. Somehow she thinks her plants are safe and sound.

Nancy Serfass

Crested Butte

"I came to Crested Butte to ski, but I stayed for the summers," says Nancy Serfass.

An accomplished gardener and garden designer, now Nancy complains of too-long winters and too-short summers for growing plants. She remembers what sparked her gardening passion despite Crested Butte's harsh weather extremes: "I would go into the meadows and come back with the colors of the wild-flowers in my head. I wanted to paint my house in those colors, but I could never find paint that would match, so I decided to grow the flowers instead."

Nancy lives in the middle of town in a cream-colored Victorian home with purple trim. Several gardens occupy the home's small backyard. Although Nancy claims that a love of chaos underlies her garden design, each garden is a graceful and well-balanced creation, composed of layers of texture, form, and color. In the corner of the yard, a whimsical metal sculpture created by local artist Shawn Guerrero presides over a terraced rock garden. The chrome-winged figure, fashioned from vacuum cleaner and car parts, dances on a large flat rock backed by willowy fireweeds and fat spikes of purple, pink, and deep plum lupines. Below the dancer, yellow poppies, blue columbines, mountain bluebells, and Jacob's ladders grow among mounds of chartreuse lady's mantle. Pink drops of bleeding heart nod on stems that arch over silver lamb's ears, pussytoes, and hot pink soapwort.

On the other side of the yard is a kidney-shaped flower bed. Around an aspen tree planted in the center, white and pink lupines form a backdrop for poppies, penstemons, and columbines. Frothy blue forget-me-nots grow next to pink clovers and orna-mental kales at the border's edge. The symmetrical grouping of plants form a perfectly tapered arch of bright colors across the trunk of the tree.

With little regard for fancy tools or the Latin names of plants ("I only remember them in rare moments of lucidity!"), Nancy only spends one hour per month maintaining her gardens during the summer, and mows all the plants to three inches in the fall. During winter, Nancy still skis, but mostly she dreams of summer, and her gardens sleeping under the snow.

Crested Butte

Great gardens can be contagious. Next door to Nancy Serfass, pansies, dianthus, sweet woodruff, and other low-growing plants flow in wide sweeps of purple, pink, and white down the berm in Char and Jim Hansen's front yard. Juniper bushes and shrubby cinquefoils grow among huge boulders at the top of the berm, and soapwort and sedums drip off rounded rocks scattered through the area. Along a fence to the side of the house, the clear, bright colors of columbines and Oriental poppies punctuate drifts of blue flax. Mountain penstemons, bluebells, and painted daisies spread among more rocks, dwarf firs, and junipers. Deep blue violas and silvery-white snow-in-summer shimmer at the border's edge.

Char collaborated with garden designer Barbara Hay to create the gardens that surround her home. Barbara, a trans-plant to Crested Butte from Zimbabwe, finds gardening in Colorado similar to her African experience. "Dianthus, wild violets, columbines, and snow-in-summer are all plants I used in gardens back home," says Barbara. "The growing conditions between parts of Zimbabwe and Crested Butte are very similar."

Barbara amended the Hansens' soil with peat moss and manure, and hand-picked the boulders and rocks from the local quarry. She chose hardy plants that would spread and evolve naturally into informal groupings for an uncultivated garden look. "I also planned the gardens to be water-efficient and self-maintaining," she says. "The plants only need infrequent but thorough soakings—the same treatment that wildflowers receive in the open meadows."

Columbines are Char's favorite wildflowers, and she added red and yellow varieties to Barbara's plantings. The mix of flowers reminds her of the beauty she encounters on hikes outside of town. Having lived in a variety of places—from Omaha to Virginia to Singapore—Char values the natural splendor and easygoing charm of Crested Butte. "Here, people regard you not for how much money you make, but for how many kayak trips you take," says Char. "The gardening is more relaxed, too. Weeds don't sprout up overnight like they do elsewhere. I only weed once every summer."

Besides the onset of winter, the other major threat to Char's garden are her puppies, Holly and Ivy. "I'm not so relaxed about that," she says.

Susan Lohr

Crested Butte

Finding Susan Lohr's home and gardens in a secluded location at 10,000 feet is like discovering a secret and enchanted world. Susan and her family live at the end of the highest road in Mount Crested Butte near the Crested Butte Ski Area. The Lohr home, Casa Rosada, is a rose-colored adobe structure they built themselves. The home is framed by the aspens crowding onto their property from Gunnison National Forest behind it. Surrounding the home are gardens that blend in seamlessly with the natural setting.

Susan was prepared for the challenges of high altitude gardening. For ten years, she lived in Gothic, a ghost town set in a high mountain meadow outside of Crested Butte. There, she served as director of the Rocky Mountain Biological Laboratory, a field station where scientists have researched a variety of topics, including plants and pollinators, since 1928. Susan remembers spectacular summers in the isolated spot and long winters when she had to snowshoe out for supplies. "It's pretty funny that I ended up here," she says, peering down the steep road winding to her home. "But I love it."

There's a lot to love, especially about gardening here, even though the growing season can be as short as six weeks. Across the front of the property, 2,000 tulips bloom in a dazzling array of colors well into August. Bright blue columbines backed by Arctic willow shrubs swarm through a high, wide berm in front of the house. Johnny jump-ups cluster around silvery lamb's ears, and pink cranesbill geraniums mix with lamium along the berm's edge. Yellow monkeyflower, a plant that grows in neighboring meadows, spreads in a puddle created by water drainage at the base of the berm.

In the backyard, Austrian copper roses and *Rosa rugosas* like 'Thérèse Bugnet' grow with Asian lilies against the warm, south-facing walls of Casa Rosada. Lacy cow parsnips lean over the back fence and blend with delphiniums, irises, and bleeding hearts in flower beds. Blue spruce, crab apple trees, and thinleaf alders circle the area.

How does Susan account for the surprising profusion and variety of plants she grows? "I take advantage of microclimates and pray there are no snowstorms in July," she says.

Buena Vista

Captivated by flowers, Barbara Pasic planted sweet peas, nasturtiums, and morning glories in her first garden when she was ten years old. It was a four-by-five foot plot near her father's vegetable garden in the mountain town of Paonia. Other childhood adventures, college, and a family of her own interrupted Barbara's gardening passion and it was years before she rediscovered the joy of growing flowers.

When Barbara and her husband, Bill, moved from Frisco to Buena Vista in 1988, they built their retirement home on two acres of horse pasture one mile west of town, with expansive picture windows deliberately designed to view future flower beds. Across the valley, Mount Princeton and the Collegiate Range added the perfect backdrop for the gardens to come.

Barbara says a pile of dirt inspired her garden design. "I garden according to how I feel. When I saw the five-foot-high mound of dirt from the excavation of the house, I said 'That's the shape I want for my garden.'"

After adding rabbit manure to the sandy soil and anchoring the dirt with lichen-covered rocks, Barbara's dream garden was in progress. Bill surprised her with rich topsoil transported from a nearby construction site. The finished product—two berms that measure eight feet across and stand five feet high—fills the Pasics' front yard with a variety of perennials,

annuals, and bulbs that bloom from June until September. Crocuses and yellow daffodils pop up first, followed by deep pink and purple tulips. As the tulips fade, columbines, coreopsis, and coral bells begin to bloom with alyssum, snapdragons, and sweetly scented stocks. Hot pink hedge roses, black-eyed Susans, and daisies swarm across the berms in midsummer.

Barbara is crazy about poppies and planted masses of delicate, red, white, and pink Shirley poppies along the front walkway and in beds under the picture windows. After the poppies fade, elegant, six-foot spikes of burgundy and royal purple lupines take over, and deep blue delphinium bloom with red lilies, pink sweet Williams, and columbines in the garden's borders.

Even in winter, the aspens, blue spruce, firs, and bristlecone pines ensure the yard is the focal point for the Pasics. Bill planted the trees to form a backdrop for a snowmobile course created for their grandchildren to enjoy.

Barbara emphasizes the importance of acclimating plants to their new garden environment before planting them. "If you take the time to get new plants used to the water and weather in your garden, they'll go gangbusters," she says.

Barbara is also adamant about the value of deadheading. She claims that early flowering perennials, like columbine and coral bells, blossom until August if wilted blooms are meticulously clipped.

Bill says that Barbara "eats, sleeps, and dreams gardening," and she doesn't deny it. "There's nothing about it I don't like. I get a great deal of satisfaction, and I'm amazed at every bloom."

Buena Vista

"How did a mining engineer become a nursery-man?" is the way Jim Ludwig began the memoir he wrote for his grandchildren. The story begins in 1950, when Jim moved from Wisconsin to manage the molybdenum mine at Climax, located at the top of Fremont Pass at 11,000 feet. While Climax was his family's home for years, the Ludwigs vacationed in Buena Vista in the Arkansas River Valley. Jim loved the area—the rolling ranchlands with mountain vistas, the mild climate, and the abundance of native plants that grew in the region's sandy soil. The contrast between Buena Vista's natural beauty and the barren landscape of Climax, which resulted from years of mining operations, started to gnaw at Jim. He began to explore ways to revegetate the Climax area.

"Most of the experts laughed," says Jim, "but I pictured fields of penstemons, scarlet gilias, and evening primroses growing with quaking aspens, spruces, and pines." His vision resulted in the purchase of a forty-acre farm in Buena Vista. Jim and his sons planted trees and high altitude shrubs like thimble-berries and whitestem gooseberries to use in reclamation projects across Colorado, and Jim became a leading spokesperson for similar efforts.

Pleasant Avenue Nursery was the natural offshoot of the Ludwig's interest in native plants. Jim and son Gary co-own the business. "Besides offering a variety of native plants—many propagated from collected seed—we collect site-specific seed for customers," says Gary. "We've reintroduced plants into mining sites, housing and commercial developments, and recreational areas."

Next door to the nursery is Jim's home and his illustrious garden of native plants. At the garden's center, the pinkish flowers of cliff *Jamesia*, or wax flower shrubs, frame nodding clusters of Virginia bluebells under a bristlecone pine. To the north, a rock garden blooms with penstemons and columbines in early summer, and prairie smoke and erigerons later in the season. White balls of pearly everlasting peer through spikes of blue-eyed grass in brick planters enclosing a patio area. Clarkia, asters, lilies, coneflowers, and black-eyed Susans mix in a colorful jumble through early fall.

"I just like to see what I can grow," Jim says, and the many Coloradans who have benefited from his reclamation efforts are glad he does.

Jamie Barron

Buena Vista

The front porch of Jamie Barron's 1927 cabin is loaded with clay pots and wooden planters overflowing with lobelias, kalanchoe, pansies, petunias, and geraniums. A chair nestled between shelves of potted plants makes a cozy place to sit and listen to the ringing of garden chimes hanging from the porch roof.

Sitting on her front porch, Jamie, who is legally blind, describes her gardening philosophy. "I'm a sun person," she says. "I like gardening because it's a way of grounding my energy and enjoying the fruits of nature."

It's not surprising then that sunflowers and giant dahlias are her favorite flowers, and that August is her favorite month. It is then that the bold perennials fill her small front yard with bright colors. Deep blue delphiniums, yellow daylilies, daisies, and veronicas also add color and crowd around the clematis-covered arch and boardwalk that lead to the front door of the log cabin and to the fragrant mock orange shrub and trumpet lilies.

Although Jamie doesn't know much about the previous owners of her cabin, tokens of their lives turn up in the garden. "The toys, marbles, and spoons I find while I'm digging are like gifts," she says.

There are, of course, more obvious gifts in Jamie's garden, like the campanulas, dianthus, Virginia bluebells, and other perennials Jamie buys at Pleasant Avenue Nursery, where her mother works. Or the trellis, boardwalk, and flower beds that a close friend, Todd Snyder, built for her.

She, however, handles the garden chores herself, creating just the atmosphere she wants. "I follow the smells and touch in the garden," she says. "I pay close attention to detail and prolong blooms with constant deadheading and trimming."

*R*idgway

It is easy to see why Ridgway, nestled in the Uncompahgre River Valley and surrounded by the majestic Cimarron and San Juan Mountains, was the chosen location for movies like *True Grit* starring John Wayne. More difficult to imagine are gardens that thrive despite the area's harsh weather conditions (a common winter temperature is minus thirty degrees Fahrenheit) and 7,000-foot elevation. Lyle Braund, manager of the Chipeta Sun Lodge in Ridgway, has proven he's up to the challenge.

Originally from Ohio where he earned a degree in landscape design, Lyle suffered allergies to midwestern plants. He now loves living and gardening in the mountains. His gardens ring the lodge and bring dimension and beauty to the already glorious surroundings. In beds that curve along the entry to the adobe structure, perennials such as penstemons, Indian paintbrush, columbines, mallows, and Mexican hat mix companionably against a backdrop of Arctic dwarf willows, Siberian pea shrubs, potentilla, and blue mist spirea. Lyle especially likes the sunflowers that tend to pop up everywhere and the dragon's blood sedums that dramatize the garden with their deep burgundy color.

In a field across from the lodge with Mount Sneffels in the background, Lyle planted aspens and a mixture of wildflower seeds along the stream that runs through the area. Flax, daisies, blanket flowers, coneflowers, corn poppies, and cosmos sparkle with dots of bright color in the clear mountain light. When snow covers the wildflower meadow, Lyle builds a twenty-foot ice sculpture on the site. "I like to watch what happens in nature," says Lyle. "In summer, I plant seeds and plants and let the garden take shape naturally. In winter, I build a structure and fill it with water, and the snow and cold create a cave of huge crystals that showcase what nature can do with ice."

In any season, Lyle's landscape is sublime. His gardens reflect his professional training, his energy, and his imagination.

Telluride

Rich Salem talks to his flowers. According to Susan Maybach, the landscape architect who designed his gardens, Rich's plants respond in a way she can't explain. "Telluride has clay soil, a harsh climate, and serious water shortages," says Susan, owner of Earth, Wind and Rock in neighboring Ridgway. "The cool summer nights are great for perennials, but it's still amazing how lush and full Rich's gardens have become. He shows what a difference an owner's involvement —weeding, watering, watching—makes in a garden."

The foliage and blossoms of trees and shrubs envelope the Salem home, located on a quiet street in the center of Telluride. Spilling over the steps to the front door are the arching branches and delicate blooms of Chinese lilac and blue mist and 'Snow White' spirea shrubs. The light purple foliage of red-leaf rose contrasts with the dark purple leaves of sandcherry shrubs, while hardy cranberry bushes and dwarf ninebark shrubs continue the parade.

In the side yard, a low wall of sandstone pavers encircles a crab apple tree. Snapdragons and campanulas jostle with pansies, edelweiss, and moneywort in a colorful potpourri at the base of the tree.

Dark and richly veined native rocks and boulders line tiered beds in the backyard. Sandcherry and 'Shubert' chokecherry shrubs grow with crab apples in beds that hover over daylilies, columbines, peonies, and delphinium. Viper's blugloss, with bristly leaves and purple bell-shaped flowers, is a prized biennial among the plantings.

Connected to more than just his own backyard, Rich Salem feels strongly about protecting the natural resources of the Telluride region. In 1994, he formed a land trust, the San Miguel Conservation Foundation (SMCF). As one of its first actions, SMCF purchased Bear Creek Canyon, a 325-acre wilderness area adjacent to the town of Telluride. The innovative partnership of public and private interests ensures that Bear Creek will never be developed.

"Everyone's garden is as important as what's out there," says Rich. "All of us have an opportunity to preserve and honor the beauty of the world around us."

Gloria Rios
Monte Vista

Gloria Rios admits she's a romantic at heart. Nowhere does her joyous spirit reveal itself more than in her garden. "I planted this garden to attract a few hummingbirds, and now look," she says, gesturing to a yard where multitudes of birds, bees, and butterflies hover over borders packed with colorful flowers.

The borders circle the backyard patio of Dos Rios Restaurant, which Gloria owns and operates with her husband Dan. Often cited as the best Mexican restaurant in the state, Dos Rios stands on Highway 112 in Monte Vista, just west of Alamosa and deep in the San Luis Valley. Situated between the Sangre de Cristo Mountains to the east and the San Juan Mountains to the west, the area around Monte Vista has spectacular beauty and a rich history that chronicles the influence of Native American, Hispanic, and Anglo cultures.

An all-white garden greets visitors to the Rios' backyard oasis. The white pom pom blooms of a snowball bush, a species of viburnum, and the small double white flowers of bridal wreath spirea make a lacy backdrop for white bee balms, white columbines, silvery lamb's ears, and snow-in-summer. A swirl of pink and white cosmos surrounds blue delphiniums in a nearby flower bed for a pleasing contrast to the silvers, whites, and grays. Across from the white garden, the sweet scent of lilacs mix with the spicy fragrance of pink and red carnations growing at the base of the shrubs. Pink yarrow, veronicas, daylilies, gaillardia, and flax grow under a 'Radiant' flowering crab apple tree in the center of the yard. Dos Rios patrons seated at tables scattered around the patio seem delighted with their surroundings. "This is what the romance of the garden is all about," says Gloria. "The garden entices people in to enjoy the flowers, and to feel good about the world and the people they're with."

The most romantic garden spot for Gloria is by the waterfall and pond that Dan built for her at the end of the yard. Vinca and potentilla ground covers blanket the area in tiny blue and yellow flowers. Dan and Gloria retire to a bench overlooking the falls to unwind after work. As the water splashes below them, they watch the sun set over the luxuriant mass of flowers crowded along the perimeter fence.

Striking groupings of plants line the fence in a steady procession. White marguerite daisies cluster among spires of deep blue delphiniums. Against the blue mist of Russian sage, the rich tones of bachelor buttons, black-eyed Susans, and asters provide an array of blue, gold, and purple. Red hot pokers and deep pink yarrow form a backdrop for pink clarkias, black pansies, and purple Corsican violas. Yellow clematis and apricot honeysuckle vines spread across the fence while the bright pink and white ruffled blooms of Shirley poppies, one of Gloria's favorite flowers, ramble along the border's edge. A hollow log brimming with moss roses, Livingstone daisies, and gazanias lays in a corner spot among mounds of 'Silver Bell' petunias. "I love the reseeding petunias and other reseeding annuals," says Gloria. "Growing

them is like raising kids. You teach them to be independent, and then when they go off on their own, you need to pull them back in."

Gloria's garden paradise was barren when she started planting flowers in 1989. "One thing that's not romantic is gardening in the arid, desert land of southern Colorado," she says. Of the many gardening tips she shares, amending the soil is at the head of Gloria's list. She adds locally processed mushroom compost to her topsoil every spring. Because she doesn't want to harm the birds and bees in her garden, and wants a safe environment where her grandchildren can play, Gloria's garden is chemical-free. She grows wild clover among perennials and annuals to provide alternate, and hopefully more attractive, tidbits for hungry garden pests. To cope with her region's intense summer heat, Gloria waters as infrequently as possible to develop the plants' tolerance for the dry, hot conditions.

Bougainvillea vines, banana trees, bromeliads, and jasmine plants grace the dining room of Dos Rios' interior. The plants remind Gloria of her mother's garden in Mexico. There are also shelves full of plants that Gloria baby-sits for customers and friends. For Gloria, romancing the garden never ends.

Center

When Karen Perrin and her husband Tom first moved from Las Vegas to the southern Colorado town of Center, she only dabbled in gardening. It started by planting a shade tree because the desert valley reminded her of the heat in Las Vegas. It became earnest when the couple moved to a house in the countryside in 1977 and began to remodel. With the house under construction, there was no place inside for Karen to be alone, so she went outside and started to plant flowers. Soon the garden became her "living palette," where she was able to express her creativity and nurture her soul.

"I think heaven is on earth," Karen says, and the Edenesque garden plots around her home are proof. It is a heaven, however, that takes a lot of time and work. When she and her husband, Tom, moved to southern Colorado, her friends said the city girl would never last. When the thermometer registered minus forty degrees Fahrenheit that first winter, she almost believed them.

Because the valley was dominated by potato farming in the late 1970s, Karen had to find alternative and creative ways to develop her garden. There were no large nurseries and few other serious gardeners in Center. Karen planted her flower beds with sweetly scented lemon lilies, some irises from her mother's garden, and plants from the few local gardeners. A lush twenty-foot strip of yellow daylilies on the west side of the Perrins' property was established from a small clump that Tom brought home from an acquaintance in nearby Saguache. When a neighbor tore lilac bushes out of his yard with a tractor and chain, Tom brought them home. In spite of her mother's certainty they would never grow, Karen's intuition led her to mulch and water them. The lilacs now bloom profusely behind the daylily plants and provide a lovely windbreak for the yard. "Maybe they are grateful," she says.

Every morning in the growing season Karen takes her coffee and strolls through her garden to "get recharged." Though protective of her privacy, she is gracious to neighbors who occasionally stop and comment on the beauty of the garden or ask advice. She believes gardens are to be shared and says, "When people compliment the garden it's akin to saying 'I like you.'"

Gracefully curving flower beds, visible from the road, attract attention with spikes of salmon lupine, maroon peonies, and vibrant blue penstemon. These ribbons of massed perennials bordering the thick green lawn give way to blue mist spirea and hardy shrub roses growing by the roadside fence. In the backyard a quiet green corner is shaded by a grove of aspen in a rolling carpet of grass surrounded by low Pfitzer junipers. Across the lawn a wide, curving walkway bordered by more perennials meanders by a quiet meditation garden. This small garden is backed

by the wall of the garden shed, an old gray cement building used in the past for storing seed potatoes (the inside walls are still marked with the tallies of the sacks for each year). A hardy clematis creeps up the wall of the shed and contributes large, deep purple flowers every year.

All of her flowers and plants are deliberately chosen. She only plants those roses that don't need covering in the winter, and especially loves the soft pink clusters of fairy roses because they bloom until the landscape freezes. Snowdrops and daffodils are the earliest flowers to appear, usually in February. In early April other bulbs begin to bloom—peony-like 'Angelique' tulips, 'Apricot Beauty', and elegant, fringed 'Burgundy Lace' tulips. Karen avoids orange colors in the garden, but she raves about the ten-inch

blooms of the yellow parrot tulips with orange veins that she says stand out and say, "Boom! Here I am."

Groundcovers flow under taller plants and shrubs throughout the garden. Coral pink soapwort, creeping 'Purple Wave' petunias, and sweet alyssum are favorites. Flowing mounds of bronze-leafed dragon's blood, autumn joy, and other varieties of sedum, including a pale green sedum with yellow, star-shaped flowers set off blue salvia, columbine, broad-leafed hostas, and lacy astilbe.

Karen integrates her natural inspirations for beautiful combinations of color and form with considerations of plant height and growing conditions. Plants in Center must adapt to fifty degree differences between day and night temperatures. Although winters seem to have tempered to lows of only minus twenty degrees, she uses plants that are hardy to minus forty degrees. One advantage of the severe cold is a natural elimination of many pests that plague gardeners in warmer climates. The soil in the garden is rich with nitrogen that seeps in from surrounding farmland, and there are very few rocks in this part of the San Luis Valley. They never use fertilizer in the flower beds, but she says, "I firmly believe in mulch." She puts all grass clippings in the garden.

Karen's advice to gardeners just starting out is to "keep it fun and follow your instincts. Flop out the garden hose and use its natural curves to shape borders or walkways and create a free-flowing design. Add interest to flat areas by creating small hills and elevating flower beds. If there's a blank spot, see what's around it and find something that fits in." Her philosophy is that you should plant your garden for yourself rather than for others. "It doesn't matter where you live, you can make it beautiful."

DELPHINIUM, 'PURPLE WAVE' PETUNIA, LUPINE, AND YARROW

LUPINE, CALIFORNIA POPPY, SEDUM, DRUMSTICK ALLIUM, VERONICA, AND PANSY

Center

Dorothy and Harold Martin have much more than a patch of sweet peas. It stretches to cover almost 200 feet of fence in front of their home near Center. It's a sight: thousands and thousands of fragrant blossoms in every shade of red, pink, white, lavender, blue, and maroon, set off by the blue mountains that enfold the San Luis Valley. The scent is incredible too, wafting on the warm, dry breeze the valley produces from June well into autumn. Tourists often stop to marvel at the row of sweet peas that grow so thickly that some confuse it for some sort of exotic shrub hedge.

The Martins have been gardening all their lives, growing both flowers and vegetables, but sweet peas are Dorothy's specialty. She laments that more gardeners don't grow them, but she thinks some people who give them a try fail because they don't understand what the annual vines require to thrive. Her secret is to dig a ten-inch trench next to the fence early in spring, work in plenty of compost, and plant it thickly. Each spring she buys three pounds of seed in mixed colors from her local seed company. A soaker hose, which ensures thorough, deep watering, runs the entire length of the fence. She doesn't skimp on the water. "They can't stand a day of drought, especially during hot weather," she says.

To keep the flowers blooming, they must be picked continuously to keep the plants from putting energy into seed production. Friends, neighbors, and passing admirers become the lucky recipients of spicily scented bouquets. Dorothy isn't afraid of the first light freezes and their effect on her sweet pea display. "They're hardy," she explains. "Most years I can pick them well into October."

The Martins are surprised that their sweet pea hedge has become a tourist attraction, but they enjoy meeting gardeners from all over the country who can't resist stopping. Dorothy was surprised when the local newspaper wanted to do a story about her and the sweet peas. "I didn't have to rob a bank to get my picture in the paper," she quips. "There I was—right next to Garfield!"

Sweet peas aren't Dorothy's only love. Stands of sunflowers, nearly thick and tall enough to be called a grove, nearly obscure their home from view of passing motorists. As much as the sweet peas need their daily pampering, the sunflowers survive with little attention or water and seed freely, even after birds have eaten their fill. "They're just the wild kind, but I think they're pretty. They come up volunteer and I don't have to worry about them," says Dorothy. "At the end of the season, I just shake off the seeds, knowing that where they drop I'll have flowers next year."

Pots of cheerful annuals are clustered near the Martins' front door. The display spills to the out-buildings behind the house. The flowers, planted in weathered wood planters, contrast effectively with the rustic fences and lead the eye to the farm fields and mountain views beyond.

Even when Dorothy can't be home tending her flowers, she has a stand-in. A clothing store mannequin (dressed in typical gardening clothes) strikes a casual pose on a bench near the front door. It's fooled many passersby into thinking Dorothy is taking a break from her chores, and the octogenarian is amused when she is confused for the Barbie doll–proportioned dummy. "They wonder how I ever get anything done sitting out there in the sun all day long," she laughs.

Pat Flynn

Beulah

The drive from Pueblo to Beulah, twenty-six miles away, is through the browns and grays of short-grass prairie to the lush green valley bordering San Isabel National Forest. Situated within the valley, Beulah is a small community in the foothills of the Wet Mountains, and has an interesting history.

In the late 1800s, the area was called Mace's Hole after outlaw Juan Mace, who hid his rustled cattle in the valley. Signal Mountain outside of present-day Beulah was where Mace and his gang sent up smoke signals to warn of trouble. When the Mace gang left the valley, residents chose the Biblical name of Beulah for their law-abiding community. With increasing civilization came a boom in Beulah's popularity as a summer retreat for Pueblo residents.

Pat Flynn spent weekends in Beulah with her family as a child. In 1990, she moved there permanently and transformed the original weed patch surrounding her brown stucco home into free-spirited cottage gardens. A garden angel perched on a post greets visitors entering the front yard. Steps lead down to the house where pots of ruffly 'Martha Washington' geraniums stand on either side of the front door. Under huge ponderosa pines, pink and rose-colored impatiens spread around pots of begonias. The trees shade picnic tables lined with pots of mint, petunias, and chartreuse licorice ferns. Yellow lilies cluster around Pat's pride and joy—a potted oleander shrub flowering in deep red blooms. Pat overwinters the tender plant on her front porch.

Stands of aspen trees fill the area on the east side of the house. Forget-me-nots and tulips bloom among the trees in spring. Apricot and white roses ramble among lavender pin-cushion flowers, cosmos, gloriosa daisies, and giant red salvias during summer months. Attracted by a birdbath surrounded with pansies, hummingbirds, orioles, finches, and yellow warblers regularly swoop through the garden. Against the fence bordering the property stand towering hollyhocks with huge purple blooms, completing the exuberant, multicolored scene.

Pat's gardening passion has spread. Up and down her street, cottage gardens sprout up, filled with blooms, flower-filled pots, and happy, chirping birds.

Beulah

Samm Carter didn't notice many gardens in Beulah when she moved to town from "the great American desert of Pueblo" in 1977. Originally from Michigan, Samm and her husband wanted a greener, quieter environment for raising their children. After purchasing a five-acre site near the San Isabel Forest, the couple began setting down roots. Samm got her husband to dig up areas for gardens before they had even unpacked. "The townspeople came out and watched this curious activity," says Samm. "They thought we were city slickers trying to grow a garden in the country."

The "activity" paid off in informal gardens that spread through the Carters' property and blend with the beauty of their natural surroundings. The garden to the north of the Carters' home is Samm's favorite. Against the distant silhouette of a weathered barn, a large cedar tree shelters pink astilbes and forget-me-nots that crowd around moss-covered rocks. Because the shaded area retains more moisture from rain and snowfall, Samm says perennials in that spot are more vigorous and more vibrant in color than anywhere else on her property. In neighboring borders, seven-foot delphiniums with spikes of brilliant blue flowers grow among hollyhocks, lupines, and columbines. The perennials form a colorful backdrop for irises and Shasta daisies.

To the west of the house, an arbor formed by the branches of a willow tree leads to a flagstone path interplanted with varieties of thyme. The fragrant

path continues to an open area filled with native buffalo grass and bordered by aspen trees, forsythia, and weeping fig shrubs. The white-veined leaves of 'Needlepoint' ivy glitter beneath the trees and shrubs. Bordering the cultivated landscape, cottonwood trees line a creek and flow into areas of scrub oak and a forest of ponderosa pines beyond.

A master gardener, Samm started a garden club in Beulah in 1990. No longer considered a gardening oddity among the locals, she now shares her tips and her passion for gardening in this unique region of the state.

$\mathscr{C}$olorado $\mathscr{P}$lateaus

The landscape of Colorado's plateau region is diverse, mysterious, often awe inspiring. Extending along the western part of the state, the region's varied ecosystems include deserts, piñon-juniper woodlands (also called pygmy forests), and valleys following the rivers that cut through the plateau. Situated at altitudes from 4,500 to about 7,000 feet, and located within different configurations of mountain ranges and mesas, the valleys of the plateau experience distinct climates and weather patterns. Readily available irrigation systems in some regions convert arid landscapes into flourishing areas of trees, vegetables, and flowers.

The Grand Junction area contains both high desert and piñon-juniper woodlands. With a scant seven inches of annual rainfall, the region is hot and dry during the growing season, and the soil varies from heavy clay to sand. Featured Grand Junction gardens are backed up against the red cliffs of the Colorado National Monument. The stark look of gnarled junipers and the muted gray-greens and silvers of native shrubs like rabbitbrush, winterfat, greasewood, and sage extend from the gardens into the surrounding landscape.

The Four Corners area to the south encompasses areas of desert, pygmy forest, and fertile, irrigated land. From Cortez, next to Mesa Verde National Park, energetic visitors can tour a red-rock canyon, skirt a 14,000-foot peak, and fish in miles of streams and small lakes—all in the same day. The featured Cortez garden sports an antique wagon brimming with deep purple verbena, alyssum, and petunias, thanks to Cortez' ample sunshine, thirteen inches of annual rainfall (the same as Denver), and mild winters. Ten miles north, the small town of Dolores, at 7,000 feet of altitude compared to Cortez' 6,200, reports annual rainfall of eighteen inches and double

the snow that its neighbor receives. Proximity to the McPhee Reservoir and the Dolores River contribute to the fertile look of the area. At Dolores' Four Seasons Nursery, Japanese maples shelter rhododendron shrubs, ferns, and orchids in shady areas while sunny spots feature Persian roses, hollyhocks, and sunflowers. Farther up the Dolores Valley, sagebrush forms a six-foot-high hedge welcoming visitors to a garden reminiscent of those in Grand Junction.

Orchards of fruit trees and farmland fill the countryside around Hotchkiss, a rural town on the Gunnison River's North Fork. The owners of Hotchkiss' Round Earth Organic Farm grow vegetables and flowers to sell at farmers' markets in Paonia, Crested Butte, and Telluride. With the West Elk Mountain Range stretching across the distant horizon, rows of tomatoes, corn, lettuce, and spinach intermix with delphiniums, baby's breath, calendulas, and nasturtiums. Although the area is dry, the climate is

mild, and the area's extensive irrigation system provides needed water. Gardeners here report a growing season extending into November.

To the southeast is Montrose, sometimes called the "doughnut hole" of the region. Protected by mountains, Montrose boasts a long growing season with balmy summers and winters of minimal snow. A short distance away, the mountain town of Ridgway experiences violent winter storms and a shortened growing season. The featured Montrose garden is an oasis of trees, roses, waterfalls, and streams set in the area's expanse of flat terrain with the San Juan Mountains in the distance. Roses—even hybrid tea varieties—thrive in gardens throughout the Western Slope, thanks to the dry, sunny climate and mild winters.

On the La Plata River west of Durango is Hesperus, another community of rolling ranch and farmland and mountain vistas. Perhaps inspired by

HESPERUS

the bounty of wildflowers filling nearby La Plata Canyon, several Hesperus gardeners have become fanatical about growing flowers. David Alford, owner of the Blue Lake Ranch Country Inn, leads the charge. David is well-known throughout Colorado for the fields of irises that blanket his property in shimmering blues and purples every spring. In addition to his passion for growing flowers, David collects and sells flower seeds. Hoping to fill his valley with flowers, he has encouraged neighbors—featured with him in this section—to embark on small-scale farming operations and plant acres of flowers, vegetables, and herbs.

Whether gardening in desert canyons with eagles flying overhead, in valleys of rivers and lakes, or in farmlands that stretch to the horizon, gardeners in Colorado's plateau regions are creating gardens as surprising, varied, and dramatic as the landscapes that surround them.

New Castle

"All I ever wanted was a bed of roses," says Rosie Ferrin.

Rosie is one of the most controversial and well-loved citizens of New Castle, a former coal-mining town located on the Great Hogback Plateau, twelve miles west of Glenwood Springs. She is referring to the white iron bed frames overflowing with roses, daisies, gaillardia, and phlox that stand in front of the old New Castle Elementary School where she lives. Along with her husband, Cleyo, Rosie bought the school when the building was about to be condemned. She then turned it into a combination dance hall, soup kitchen, art gallery, and stone grotto with hot tub on the first floor, and affordable housing on the second. Ultimately, Rosie envisions the yellow brick school as a gathering place for writers, artists, and gardeners.

The gardens that sprawl over the school grounds are equally ambitious. Newcomers driving past the Main Street location jolt upright at the sight of the vast and unusual plantings. Along the front of the school, each flower-filled bedstead stands at the head of a long raised flower bed lined with logs. These flower beds are also home to old wagons and antique milk jugs filled with pansies, geraniums, and petunias that are in turn surrounded by plants of every size, shape, and color. Feathery pink bee balms, astilbes, and blue pincushion flowers jostle among spikes of deep purple veronicas. Huge columbines roam through obedient plants, mallows, and black-eyed Susans. Among the sea of blooms, thick masses of lupines and coneflowers support delphiniums that rise from their midst. Roses climb on electrical wires that drape over the beds.

More roses twine over arches made of conduit pipe and chicken wire that stand at either end of the front gardens. One arch leads to Cleyo's vegetable garden on the school's west side. Cucumbers, zucchini, tomatoes, and corn grow in raised beds guarded by rows of brightly colored hollyhocks. On the building's east side, snow-on-the-mountain, ajugas, and lamium spread among the hopeful new plants in Rosie's experimental gardens. Describing herself as "Monet in rebellion," Rosie says she just can't stop adding more flowers to her already dizzying array of blooms.

Rosie has a deep connection to her garden. She left her native country, the Philippines, during the Marcos regime. Tending a garden is like having her family back again, she says, and she refers to her flowers as her babies. "Actually, my flowers are better than kids," Rosie says. "If you take care of them, they don't leave you, and they don't talk back."

Rosie's maternal instinct for her plants has resulted in clashes with New Castle's City Council. Despite city-imposed watering restrictions, Rosie insists that her plants must have additional water to survive. During summer months, local newspapers regularly feature photographs of Rosie—dressed in a muumuu and her head wreathed in flowers—watering her garden with water from the ranch that she and Cleyo own outside of town. "The city should thank me," says Rosie. "With all the development in New Castle, my garden is providing the extra oxygen we need. I wish every new resident would bring a tree with them."

New Castle's mayor, Steve Rippy, agrees that the town is booming. A bedroom community serving towns like Aspen, a two-hour drive away, New Castle's population has more than doubled since

1990. With the water treatment plant in this semi-arid region working at maximum capacity, New Castle instituted reduced hours in the mornings and evenings for watering lawns and gardens. Colorado State University educators held classes for area residents, explaining that watering during the early morning and evening hours—when less evaporation takes place—was more efficient, and ultimately more beneficial for plants.

Rosie disagrees.

"The town tickets me for watering my plants," says Rosie, "but there's enough water for car washes. Can washing a car be more important than watering my flowers?'"

Grand Junction

Arlen and Virginia Beemer's home, located in a subdivision outside of Grand Junction, is set against the stark splendor of the Colorado National Monument. Some of the monument's mammoth sandstone formations, sculpted into fantastic shapes by wind and water over millions of years, practically sit in the Beemers' backyard. From their patio, Arlen sees the craggy profiles of Indian chiefs and Easter Island natives jutting from the cliff walls. Virginia looks for eagles and hawks that sail across the canyon and delights in the quail with feathery topknots that perch on the garden walls.

"After college, we looked long and hard for the place we wanted to be and this was it. Thirty years later, the desert, the mountains, the dryness still captivate us," says Arlen.

The Beemers' adobe home and gardens of native trees and plants reflect their love and reverence for the canyonlands. The muted gray-greens and silvers of junipers and piñons and shrubs like rabbitbrush, winterfat, greasewood, and sage dot the surrounding landscape and extend into their gardens. Indian paintbrush, wild hyssop, and prickly pear cactus are some of the native perennials that grow among the shrubs and trees. Arlen is enthusiastic about the plants he's grown from seed gathered on the monument—like yucca that blooms in large clusters of white flowers. Salvias, veronicas, and bright yellow Missouri primroses spread around the curl-leaf mountain mahogany and desert holly shrubs that also grew from seed.

A wash runs across the front of the Beemers' property and wildflowers like scarlet gilia, paper flower, Indian blanket, and penstemons thrive in the moister soil. A specimen Scotch broom plant with arching stems of bright yellow flowers stands by the front entry alongside a manzanita, a shrub with crooked branches and smooth red bark that Arlen nurtured from a Denver Botanic Garden seedling. At the other side of the entry a sandcherry explodes with white blooms in the spring. The tree was a gift from the Beemers' daughter, a botanist and nursery-woman who is still amazed at the way the original container plant has taken off.

A grape arbor leads to the rear of the house where Arlen created a brick patio with a small sunken pond surrounded by roses. He built an adobe wall that curves along the perimeter of the area and echoes the sweeping lines of the monument's cliffs looming beyond. To soften the look of the stark adobe, he planted rose-pink desert four o'clocks along the wall's base. Yarrow, blue flax, and grasses like northern oats and Indian ricegrass drift through the yard behind the patio and seem part of the natural landscape. With all the beauty he has created around him, Arlen points out a huge gnarled juniper at the far side of the patio. He guesses the tree is between three and four hundred years old. "When my father first visited and saw the tree, he thought it must be sick and wanted to help me cut it down," says Arlen. "But he's lived all his life in eastern Kansas and doesn't identify with the unique feeling of the desert. This tree is my favorite part of the garden. When I build a deck here I'll wrap it around the juniper so the tree really stands out."

Amending the soil with peat and installing a drip irrigation system are ways the Beemers have met the growing challenges of their dry, hot climate. But Arlen feels the most important element to any garden is its harmony with the environment.

"Get a feel for where you are," he says simply. "Then plant what fits."

Tony and Allison Richards

Grand Junction

Grand Junction landscape architect Ann Barrett couldn't believe her ears when she got the call from Tony and Allison Richards. A proponent of native landscaping, Ann usually had to try to sell the idea of using drought-tolerant plants to potential clients. The Richards actually wanted to create a landscape plan that fit in with the desert feeling of their home.

Living next door to the Beemers at the base of the Colorado National Monument with the Book Cliffs stretching to the west and the Grand Mesa to the east, the Richards shared the same dramatic backdrop and many of the same growing challenges as their neighbors. The couple was eager to learn about gardening in their area and to participate in the landscape planning process. Ann was more than happy to comply.

"Grand Junction gets an average of seven inches of rain per year, half of what Denver receives," says Ann. "The area around the National Monument was the bottom of an ancient ocean, so the soil is often heavy and very alkaline, almost like concrete. Add relentless heat to the equation and you have a very tough growing environment. By utilizing the grasses, trees, shrubs, bulbs, and plants that thrive here, however, you can create gardens of incredible beauty and interest that are unlike anywhere else. They are simply out of this world."

The lush gardens surrounding the Richards' home prove the point. Blue mist spirea, gaillardia, evening primroses, coreopsis, and yarrow fill beds on either side of the entryway. Tufts of blue fescue pop up at intervals. Junipers, firs, and a variety of native shrubs and trees provide structure to the plantings. Allison loves the three-leaf sumacs with cone-shaped clusters of flowers in summer, followed by red berries and brilliant red foliage in the fall.

A drainage problem resulted in one of the Richards' favorite garden areas. By diverting water that was flowing close to the house foundation into an area to the side of the house, they created a swale where wildflowers and native grasses flourish. A dry wash filled with smooth rocks leads through blue flax, verbena, penstemons, scarlet globemallows, and little bluestem and Indian ricegrasses to the backyard.

A bridge arches over the wash to a tiled swimming pool surrounded by beds filled with lilies, penstemons, black-eyed Susans, and shrub roses. With its hot days, cool nights, and dry air that discourages pests and mildew, the canyonlands provide a perfect climate for growing roses that are spectacular all summer long. Ann favors the David Austin and Canadian roses for their hardiness and long bloom.

Beyond the pool, steps lead up to a small patio sheltered by an arch. Here the Richards sit with their family and friends and take in the wild beauty of the National Monument and its surroundings. Yucca, Mormon teas, and Apache plumes are some of the desert plants that the Richards brought into their garden landscape. "We try to mimic what we see on the monument in our yard," says Allison. Unfortunately, there is more to the desert than its plants, and Allison admits that she and Tony sometimes spot mountain lion tracks on their frequent walks.

Masses of purple coneflower hold court in beds closer to the house. The perennials are backed by dwarf ninebark, serviceberry, and alpine currant shrubs. Around the corner is Tony's vegetable garden. Lettuce, tomatoes, beans, potatoes, artichokes, snow peas, and Anaheim and habanero peppers are only some of the vegetables he grows in long raised beds.

Ann refuses to take credit for the Richards' desert paradise. "I birthed the landscape plan. Allison and Tony nurtured it and made it grow into the gardens you see today."

Susan and Gene Alexander

Whitewater

In the early morning when the birds start singing, Susan Alexander thinks her garden is the best place on earth. Susan and her husband Gene live and garden in a valley outside of Whitewater, south of Grand Junction. Their property borders the Grand Mesa National Forest. Purdy Mesa dominates the landscape, and Kannah Creek runs behind the house. The Alexanders have found arrowheads and the remnants of fire pits on their land, evidence of a Ute Indian campground. Susan has heard that Kannah is a Ute word for water.

A Colorado State University master gardener, Susan works for the Book Cliffs Nursery in Grand Junction. She is excited about the many new varieties of plants available for her hot and dry growing region. Her personal motto, "When a plant comes in, take it home," is reflected in the prolific gardens that surround her home. In the front yard, an orchard of peach and apricot trees borders a vegetable garden where corn, tomatoes, asparagus, and peppers grow in raised beds. Susan mashes her habanero peppers into a spray that she applies to tulips to deter nibbling deer in the spring. Raccoons, rabbits, and chipmunks are some of the other garden pests she battles.

Susan relies on trees to pull her garden design together. Aspen, spruce, black walnut, gambel oak, and hickory trees skirt the perimeter of perennial beds that line a small oval of lawn. Because Susan experiments with plants uncommon to her area, gladiolus and cleome mix with the more familiar hollyhock, Rocky Mountain penstemon, and bee balm. Bright red crocosmia partners with veronicas, statice, daisies, gilias, and coreopsis in waves of color that flow through the heart of the flower beds. White and blue bellflowers along with hot pink dianthus form a pleasing and long-lasting border. Climbing along a nearby lattice is a 'Gold Flame' honeysuckle vine. Its rich fragrance wafts through the garden.

The Alexanders' favorite tree is the weathered juniper that leans over the creek behind their home. The glossy green leaves of Oregon grape and holly spread under the tree and down the bank. Ferny leadplant with stalks of purple flowers mingles with barberry, western sandcherry, and santolina, or lavender cotton shrubs, closer to the house. Gray-green sage grows wild in this quiet spot. "I let the sage grow naturally throughout the yard," says Susan. "I love the way its color makes a soft backdrop for the other plants. The shrubs smell wonderful after it rains."

A jumble of sage, junipers, and ponderosa pines surround the bird-watching patio where the Alexanders relax and view the chickadees, goldfinches, mountain bluebirds, and golden eagles that fly through the area. When Gene isn't watching the birds, he's carving them out of basswood and butternut in a home workshop. "Around here, if I'm not carving, I'm weeding, and vice versa," Gene says with a laugh.

Amending the soil, watering, and planting—especially in the spring before the onslaught of intense summer heat shrivels new plants—are other gardening chores the Alexanders share. "Our soil is part sand, part Mancos shale," says Susan. "There is no humus in the shale, and it's impossible to break down. We rototill like crazy and add every amendment we can think of—leaves, hay, compost. The most important gardening tip for our area is to use drought-tolerant plants and then restrict watering. You can drown plants meant to survive desert conditions."

Susan claims she didn't start her garden with any particular vision; it just evolved. And grew. And got better every year.

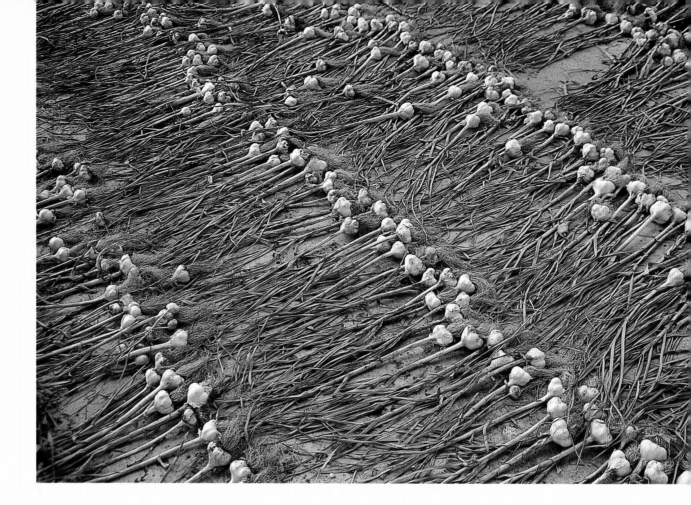

*H*otchkiss

In 1995, a group of third graders visited the Round Earth Organic Farm. Located in Hotchkiss, a community south of the Grand Mesa and west of the West Elk Mountains, Round Earth grows fruit, vegetables, and flowers to sell at farmers' markets in Paonia, Crested Butte, and Telluride. As the children wandered among the rows of vegetables and flowers, the farm's co-owner Valerie Stone asked a boy if he'd like to try some spinach. When the boy turned up his nose, Valerie offered a leaf from a nearby plant for him to try. After one bite, the child cried out to his teacher: "Hey, where can I get more of this spinach stuff?" The story is one of Valerie's favorites, and it underlies the gardening philosophy she shares with her husband Adam.

"People have forgotten where their food comes from," says Valerie. "So many have lost the connection with the earth—with what's real and meaningful."

Adam and Valerie met at the Homeless Garden Project in Santa Cruz, California. Adam was the project director, and Valerie was a teaching intern looking for hands-on ways to teach science to elementary students. The project's farm was the perfect place for Valerie's students to learn about growing food firsthand. The project also employed the homeless to grow and harvest top quality organic food for the community. "I liked the contrast of homeless people feeding the general population," says Adam.

In 1992, Adam decided to embark on his own small-scale farming, large-scale gardening venture. He visited Hotchkiss at the suggestion of friends and was immediately attracted to the wide, open valley with the long sweep of the West Elk Mountains in the distance. Thanks to plentiful water from the north fork of the Gunnison River, snowmelt from the Grand Mesa, and irrigation projects built in the early 1900s, ranches and fruit orchards had long filled the valley. Adam knew he had found the right place for his farm. He purchased ten acres of a hay farm and set to work. Valerie joined him the following year.

"Creating diversity is the key to our gardening success," says Adam. "When too many plants of one kind are planted together, there's an imbalance that results in unhealthy plants and problems with insects and birds."

Two-hundred-foot-long rows of vegetables alternating with rows of flowers and herbs line two acres of Adam and Valerie's property. Peppers, artichokes, cabbage, corn, tomatoes, and lettuce grow alongside daisies, delphiniums, baby's breath, larkspur, yarrow, clarkia, and dill. The plants—mostly from Johnny's of Maine seed—are grown for a variety of uses. The flowers end up in bouquets, wreaths, and dried flower arrangements. The petals of calendulas and nasturtiums are used in salad mixes. Thanks to a contract with Gerber's, melons and butternut squash are earmarked for baby food. Braids of garlic are popular items at area markets. An orchard of peach, plum, cherry, and apricot trees yields fruit that is coveted throughout the Western Slope.

Amending their soil was one of Adam and Valerie's biggest challenges. Besides double digging composted chicken manure, granulated rock, gypsum, and rock phosphate into the hard clay, the couple grow "green manure," which is a cover crop like buckwheat. The crops are planted in midsummer and dug back into the soil in fall before flowering. The fibrous texture of the grains creates a rich, loose loam. "Your arm will sink to the elbow when you reach down into that soil," says Adam.

The striking landscape of trees, plants, and mountain panoramas is accented by teepees scattered across Round Earth. Adam and Valerie like the picturesque quality of the structures, and use them to lodge guests and summer interns. "The interns come for farm work in the open air and a teepee over their heads at night," says Valerie.

With its abundance of food for body and soul, Round Earth is the place where Adam and Valerie's dreams have come full circle.

Montrose

Fred Maxted

A six-foot, curving hedge of 'Austrian Copper' roses ends in a stand of black pines enclosing a quiet, shady space in Fred Maxted's garden. These "sweeping curves, enticing paths, and secluded nooks" are his favorite garden feature. All the paths in the garden lead to a cloistered patio where many varieties of irises, daylilies, and roses mix together on berms. Ten white firs bring structure to the garden. Fred especially likes white fir because of its soft needles, columnar shape, and resistance to pests. He rescued nine of the ten white firs from a nursery in Ridgway after deer had damaged them. The evergreens provide year-round beauty while in spring, crab apple, decorative pear, and Nanking cherry trees bloom in varying shades of pink and white. Lavender lilacs spread around a large Arctic willow.

It's a lush landscape that provides a refreshing contrast to the flat desert surrounding it in Montrose's western plateau region. Montrose is known as the "doughnut hole" because storms in the region tend to settle in the Elk Mountains and on the Uncompahgre Plateau on either side of the valley. As a result, snow and rainfall are scarce, but thanks to extensive irrigation, Fred has plenty of water for his many plants.

130

He has compensated for the alkaline soil by using bermed beds and amending the soil with a mixture of silt and sawdust. He cautions that it is important to flatten the tops of berms before planting to keep water from draining off too fast. River rocks placed on the slopes of the berms also help retain water.

Fred, a former art teacher, didn't have a master plan when he started his garden in 1990. Instead, he approached its design as an artist would a painting—a constant refining of technique and layering of color and contrast. On a single acre, his labyrinths of pebbled pathways wind around and through islands of perennials, shrubs, and evergreens. The bits and pieces of the garden were inspired by travels to landscapes all over the world. The dense and varied foliage that Fred admired in the South Pacific and the way trees and shrubs were grouped at Butchart Gardens in British Columbia are a few of the elements he's incorporated into his own garden design. But while Fred modeled his ideas after the world's outstanding gardens, he has created an original forest that resembles no other place on earth.

The garden is not, however, simply the result of deliberate planning. Improvisation has also played a part. "I had the excavated dirt from the house construction bulldozed into mounds of dirt here and mounds of dirt there, with canyons in between. Then I looked to see what plants could be combined into a composition."

He is currently expanding the perimeter of the existing garden with xeriscaping that expresses what he calls his "free-spirited" planting. Here irises grow in a bed of river rock leading to a series of delicate waterfalls. Past the waterfalls, a path leads to an area where Fred plans to install a long arcade of climbing roses and vines that will lend a Japanese flavor to the garden. The plan is the perfect extension of Fred's singular vision—one of worldly perspective and creative tension.

Dolores

Joy and Larry Keeling started their wholesale nursery business to get Joy out of an office job. Larry says his engineering background gave him "the advantage of not knowing what he couldn't do," while the nursery business allowed Joy the chance to use her degree in horticulture. Since 1982, the couple has established twelve greenhouses and a five-acre arboretum. Retail customers come from as far as Telluride and Pagosa Springs to choose from the hundreds of varieties of drought-tolerant and native plants at the Four Seasons Nursery.

The Keelings wanted to educate their customers on gardening techniques suited for their hot, dry region, but that also meant adapting some plants to the native environment. Dolores' hard-packed, alkaline soil makes growing most trees almost impossible, so Larry places trees on top of the ground and creates berms of rich soil around the root ball. By the time the roots grow through the rich medium to the clay soil, they have become strong enough to withstand the more unforgiving soil. All of the display gardens are planted in raised beds, ensuring plants thrive in the loamy topsoil.

Both Joy and Larry are partial to trees. Joy's favorite tree is the white fir, but she also recommends globe Navajo willows as fast-growing, hardy trees that do well in shade. Larry loves 'Autumn Blaze' maples with rich green leaves turning orange-red in fall, and 'Shubert' chokecherries with leaves turning to dark red-purple in summer. Dwarf black locusts, larches, filberts, and bald cypresses are more trees found at the arboretum.

A gray stone wall separates the commercial area from the Keelings' private yard. A stream that Larry created from an irrigation ditch runs through a garden shaded by a lacy-leafed Japanese maple, redbud trees, and eastern dogwoods. A giant blue hosta flourishes by the stream's edge, along with coral bells, creeping Jenny, Japanese painted ferns, and Chinese ground orchids. Willowy miscanthus grasses weave through the plantings. Joy especially likes the glossy-leafed rhododendron shrubs that produce azalea-like flowers in the spring, and the heathers that begin blooming along the stream in February.

In front of the Keelings' log home is a 'Hoopsii' blue spruce, a variety of Colorado spruce with striking ice blue foliage. Behind the spruce, David Austin roses bloom with creamy pink flowers along a split-rail fence. Llamas stroll in a pasture bordering more garden areas. Against a backdrop of silver lace and native hop vines growing along the pasture fence, the blue mist of Russian sage floats among fireweeds, yarrows, and globe thistles.

Purple clusters of wisteria flowers cover an arbor that leads to demonstration gardens. In spring, brightly colored daffodils and tulips grow among deep blue, yellow, and pink irises. White bleeding hearts, an unusual variety, bloom against the rich colors of Japanese anemones. During summer months, the bright yellows of Persian roses and coreopsis contrast with the blue-greens of spruce trees and the dark rusty reds of barberry bushes. Hollyhocks, sunflowers, and coneflowers continue the show of color into late summer. The bright reds and oranges of sumac shrubs sweep through the gardens in the fall.

In the fall, the Four Seasons staff invites clients and neighbors to the nursery for Octoberfest. A maze of 600 straw bails is erected for the children, and craft artisans exhibit herbs, weaving, pottery, and dried flower arrangements. Christmas is celebrated with a display of 1,200 luminarias grouped with poinsettias that create a holiday glow around the greenhouses while visitors stroll among fifteen lavishly decorated evergreen trees, enjoying choral music.

It is obvious that the Four Seasons Nursery provides much more than plants; it has become a treasured resource for residents of the Four Corners area.

Karen Holmgren

Dolores

Karen Holmgren, a landscape designer and artist, sees a "symbiotic relationship" between her garden and the art she creates in her studio. The Dolores resident built her art studio on a slope at the perimeter of her garden. The studio's natural wood construction and simple lines blend with the tall native sage and scrub oak that surround her home and garden.

Karen says that gardening is a pleasant break from the intellectual discipline of her artwork. In her studio, she deliberates over the designs of her abstract sculptures, composed of hardwoods gathered from a local woodworker, branches she finds at the base of cottonwood trees, and pieces of old metal that she scouts from area junkyards.

"I am the master in my studio but in the garden I am the servant," she says. Karen accepts the designs nature offers her, rather than trying to control the natural landscape. But like any gardener, she delights in tinkering with the landscape, adding new varieties of native plants, and experimenting with different plant locations.

The lush green landscapes of her native California inspired Karen's first attempts at gardening in Dolores. When she moved to the Four Corners area in 1975, there was no local nursery, so Karen settled for the offerings of the local discount stores along with some seeds and plants from her husband's grandmother. By 1984 she was working for the new Four Seasons Nursery where owners Joy and Larry Keeling introduced her to the many native plants of southwestern Colorado. Soon Karen was testing varieties of artemisia, salvia, and yarrow, and creating native landscapes for nursery customers.

In her own yard, Karen used the big sagebrush growing throughout her property as a background for her garden and to form an archway that leads to her yard from the gravel driveway. Not only does Karen appreciate the look and fragrance of sage, but she values the plants as a deterrent to deer, which won't jump the six-foot-tall wall of sage because they can't see what is on the other side.

Between the garden and the house, a combination of green fescue grasses provide a contrast to the many hues of gray in the garden. Beyond the rich green of the lawn to the south are clary sage, blue fescue, Mexican privet, and ribbon grasses that blend with the native mountain mahogany, scrub oak, milkweed, and rabbitbrush. Soft purple lavender and catmint in the lower border complement the silvery leaves of artemisia, wormwood, and prairie sage.

To provide midsummer moisture for the blue mist spirea and gloriosa daisies that thrive in one of the hottest spots of the garden, Karen placed three-foot-square cement pads between the tall sage boundary and the garden plants. Each pad dips slightly in the center to collect water. The mini-reservoirs hold water long enough to humidify the plants, but not so long that they allow mosquitoes to breed. The handsome and functional squares in the garden echo the combination of man-made and organic forms in her studio work.

Karen's favorite month is September, when the sage's abundant blue flowers mix with masses of golden rabbitbrush blooms. Bright yellow Maximillian sunflowers and the yellow fall foliage of cottonwoods add more glowing color to the fall landscape.

"The light shining among the plants is gorgeous in the fall," says Karen. "But that just goes to show it's nature's garden, not mine."

Cortez

Tammy Haley's love of gardening began in her hometown of Rico, a small mining community north of Cortez. She remembers her Aunt Ann's spectacular roses growing in Rico's barren, rocky soil thanks to the addition of hand-hauled buckets of mine tailings.

The lesson was well-learned. When Tammy and Steve moved to Cortez from a farm five miles out of town, they brought twenty truckloads of rich farm dirt with them. Tammy describes the dirt as so fertile "you could grow pineapples in it." A yard full of beautiful annuals and perennials later, Tammy has proved that amending the soil is the key to successful gardening anywhere.

The centerpiece of Tammy's garden is an antique wagon she got "for a steal" from a friend. It is also her most prized possession. "My husband and I wrote in the contract for our house that I would never leave without that wagon," Tammy says. Understanding Tammy's passion, Steve moved the wagon to the middle of the front yard in a flatbed truck. He then fashioned a redwood planter in the wagon's interior that Tammy filled with her favorite flowers.

Tammy's love of bold, vibrant color is evident throughout her yard. Red and gold gaillardias mix with deep purple miniature delphiniums and the airy white blossoms of gaura under a juniper tree. Golden daylilies spill out of whiskey barrels standing by the front door. The sunflower seeds that Tammy plants every October stand like sentries along the driveway. In the middle of a grouping of 'Peace' roses is a bronze plaque that reads:

"Wonders spring from tiny seeds,
  Beauty from the thorn.
  So many lovely mysteries are in a garden born."

What has been born is much more than just the bright display of purple verbenas surrounded by pink and purple petunias, daisies, and alliums. Her garden causes heads to turn in Cortez and now, up and down the Haleys' block, newly inspired gardens sparkle in the bright sun.

Suzy McCleary

Hesperus

Waterfalls spill down the cliffs of La Plata Canyon, west of Durango. Mountain bluebells, false hellebores, Queen Anne's lace, larkspurs, and penstemons combine in a dizzying swirl of color and form to the sides of the falls and across the fields at their base. It is spectacular country, and to Suzy McCleary, it is an inspiration.

Having grown up near Yosemite National Park with parents and grandparents who savored the surrounding countryside and created gardens to match, Suzy fell in love with Hesperus, a rural town at the mouth of La Plata Canyon. Working at the Blue Lake Ranch, a Hesperus bed-and-breakfast noted for its sprawling, beautiful gardens, inspired Suzy to plant her own gardens, and to start a business based on the plants she loved to grow. Her Clearwater Farm provides dried flowers, soaps, herbs, seeds, and vegetables for customers lucky enough to know of her fresh products. Just walking through the Clearwater Farm gardens is a unique and rare pleasure.

Resident peacocks and geese waltz through a willow twig archway to the main garden area in front of Suzy's home. Daylilies, columbines, penstemons, daisies, and lupines grow at the edge of a pond fed by the La Plata River. Behind the log home, a dirt path leads through scrub oaks and native shrubs to a series of clearings that open onto gardens filled with flowers, herbs, and vegetables. Towering sunflowers surround the first opening where poppies and bachelor buttons scramble through feathery baby's breath

and cosmos against a backdrop of rosy pink hollyhocks. As the path leads deeper into the twelve-acre property, wild roses, gilias, penstemons, and larkspur appear among native grasses. Another clearing reveals gaillardia, iris, calendula, lavender, zucchini, and lettuce surrounded by sturdy delphiniums and aspen trees. The path loops through the woods and more gardens to the Clearwater Farm shop.

Among the abundance of plants she grows, Suzy loves sweet peas the best. Her grandfather used to grow the flowers in Wyoming, and coffee cans filled with sweet peas were a common gift.

"He's my hero," says Suzy. "He was a simple man who lived a simple life."

With her wildly beautiful, totally organic farm and natural products, Suzy has done her grandfather proud.

Hesperus

"I guess I overplanted," says David Alford as he stands before fields of pink, white, purple, yellow, and cream hollyhocks stretching off into the far distance. Then he laughs. His self-deprecating joke is pretty funny, because overplanting is David's way of life—a way of life he cherishes and exults in. The joyful abundance and profusion of the gardens surrounding his Blue Lake Ranch bed-and-breakfast are only one reflection of his passion for watching things grow—and spread.

David knew nothing about gardening when he bought 500 acres of land in rural Hesperus in 1978. At the time, he was a clinical social worker living in Durango and looking for a new direction in life. The first sight of Blue Lake with its backdrop of the La Plata Mountains convinced him that he'd found his true destination. A cattle ranch at the time of purchase, David first established a truck farm on the property, then gradually implemented his dream of a bed-and-breakfast.

With the help of his wife Shirley, a family physician who grew up on a neighboring ranch, David transformed the original dilapidated ranch house into the main house of a gracious country inn. The bright yellow clapboard structure houses four beautifully appointed guest rooms, an open kitchen, dining area, and parlor. Paths lead from the main house to five yellow cottages with different outlooks —lake, river, mountain, forest—but all with views of the beautiful grounds.

"I planted my first gardens to add more touches of beauty for my guests," says David. "The first seed I threw out was a variety of lilac from the Nature Conservancy."

The seed took—and so did the many more seeds and bulbs that followed. As a result, explosions of color and form surround the guest areas and all the areas in between on the three acres surrounding the main house.

Spring launches the first wave of overplanted splendor. In a flat field beyond the main house, huge

sweeps of blue and purple irises stretch out in a dazzling iridescence that leaves many a savvy horticulturist slack-jawed and speechless. The famous collection stems from a friendship between the couple and Dr. Jack Durrance, a renowned iris expert and hybridizer from Denver. One of Shirley's former professors, Jack invited the couple to view his massive iris plantings. When he realized their unique interest in his plants, Jack gradually passed on more and more irises to grace the Blue Lake property. In the same spirit, David and Shirley sponsor an event every June where neighbors come to Blue Lake to dig up irises for their own gardens. "You don't garden just for yourself," says David. "It's meant to be shared."

Bouquets of fresh-cut flowers adorn every public area and guest room at Blue Lake Ranch. Guests are also encouraged to cut flowers, and David and Shirley leave scissors on top of gate posts for employees to reap their own bounty. Luckily, there are more than enough to share. Bleeding hearts, columbines, daisies, and wallflowers backed by shrub roses, and lilac and spirea shrubs surround cottages and line pathways during early summer. Thousands of tulips, daffodils, and alliums spread across the fields and around Blue Lake. David and Shirley love poppies, and the yellow and orange Iceland varieties and ruffled pastel Shirley poppies are sprinkled throughout the plantings. Flanders poppies, the couple's favorite, bloom in scarlet splashes among the fields of irises. David worries that his friend Jack Durrance's purist sensibilities will be offended by the mix, but visitors' delight in the striking lines of red and purple against the long blue horizon keeps the poppies and irises as permanent Blue Lake mates.

Then there are the peonies. David can barely speak of the huge, fragrant blossoms without first burying his face in their midst. "I love peonies," he says, once he can disengage himself. With the 7,400-foot altitude and cool night air, the perennials flower well into the summer months.

During mid to late summer, more perennials take center stage at Blue Lake Ranch. Draped against the yellow walls of the main house, deep purple clematis heightens the delicacy of *Salvia turkestanica*, spiking in swirls of opalescent color. White larkspur and bachelor buttons line the white picket fence twined with clematis in hues of pink and fuchsia that circle the area. In borders to the side of the house, frothy Queen Anne's lace, hollyhocks, and Rocky Mountain penstemons wander among the hot colors of red bee balms, orange and yellow trumpet lilies, sunflowers, and calendulas. Grass paths wind through the area, which is filled with apple and peach trees.

"Garden design is something that comes to me in semi-sleep," says David. "Basically, I throw out

seeds, and if the tall plants grow to the front and the short to the back, so be it. At the main house, I planted flowers so they'd show well looking out the windows into the yard. When they also looked good from the yard, I thought, 'Hey, that's great, too!'"

All David's gardens share this multi-dimensional aspect. From every viewing angle, there is some new combination of plants to admire, some new surprise to discover. Sticking to perimeters is not the only way to experience the gardens, either. At the tiny River House, a guest cottage close to the La Plata River, David encourages guests to walk into the forest of hollyhocks towering in the side yard. "Standing among them, you can really enjoy their fragrance, their shape, their hollyhock-ness," says David. "It's also a great place to play hide-and-seek."

Ensuring that plants endure and thrive outside his own gardens is perhaps David's greatest passion. Seeds David collected of the wildflower, sweet rocket, have found their way into gardens all over Hesperus (a fitting home for a plant whose Latin name is *Hesperis matronalis*). He collects seed from his own and friends' gardens, from the surrounding countryside, and the southwest region at large. In a large log barn set in a meadow near David and Shirley's home, collected seeds are cleaned and stored and packaged for distribution. Colorful packets of sweet rockets, calendulas, bachelor buttons, hollyhocks, Flanders poppies, and cottage garden mixes are for sale at the main house. The barn itself, with a broad terrace overlooking a meadow and lines of alder and western poplar trees, is available for weddings, dances, and special events.

Gardening in the rocky soil of this glacial moraine region gives David a deep respect for "manure, water, and mulch." His other gardening axiom is, "If you have a dollar, spend ninety cents on soil and ten cents on plants."

That other more elusive ingredient for gardening success—an intuitive understanding of how plants are best displayed—is what sets David apart. His unique talent and vision are surpassed only by his love for the plants he grows.

Linda and Trent Taylor

Hesperus

Linda and Trent Taylor garden by the acre. Sheets of yellow and blue surround their home in Hesperus where they have planted 800 acres of safflowers and ten acres of bachelor buttons. An additional one thousand red gladiolus, half an acre of calendulas, three-quarters of an acre of cosmos, and an acre of four o'clocks encompass what the young couple have created in the space of one short year.

The Taylors have embarked on a large-scale organic vegetable and flower operation with the support and encouragement of their good friend, David Alford, whose Blue Lake Ranch is just down the road. David wants everyone in Hesperus to grow flowers so he can enjoy them everywhere he goes—not just in his own flower-filled backyard. The Taylors are happy to help David with his dream since it fits in perfectly with their own. As they watch their three young children decorate teepees of dried lupine stalks with petunias and marigolds, Trent and Linda talk about their new venture.

"My family has farmed wheat, oats, alfalfa, and pinto beans in this valley for generations," says Trent. "Linda and I wanted to do something different that allowed us to enjoy things a little more and to take the time to stop and look around. As Mormons, family is very important to us. Now we are able to share our lives more completely with our kids."

Linda gestures to the wide expanse of blue sky over their rolling fields and adds, "We named our business Blue Horizons Farm because it's a new start for us and because that's what we see all around us. If we have a bad day, all we have to do is go and pick some flowers, and everything falls into place."

Visitors to Blue Horizons wander through long rows of vegetables, herbs, and flowers and pick what they want, then pay at the house. In beds and rows and acres that stretch across their property, the many plant choices combine in a delight to the senses. The

earthy fragrances of cilantro, chamomile, parsley, and basil float over beds bursting with gigantic gourds of squash, watermelons, and cantaloupes. Lemony creeping thyme grows between stepping stones that lead through beds of annuals and perennials. Flowers for drying like red and white strawflower, purple-blue statice, and globe amaranth blooming in papery pink balls mix with African and painted daisies and dwarf sunflowers. In a circular mound close to the house, bright yellow daylilies jostle for space with blue delphiniums, lupines, larkspur, and white and lilac bellflowers. Across the surrounding fields, irises spread among colorful masses of wild-flowers. The bulbs and seeds come from David Alford.

"We've helped David, too," says Linda. "When deer ate all of David's self-seeding petunias in the spring, he thought his crop was lost for good—but David had donated some of those plants to our kids' school fund-raiser, and we'd bought a few flats. We gave him back a bunch of the petunia seed, and his strain of plants was saved."

Now the Taylors propagate their own plants from seed in a greenhouse donated by neighbor Suzy McCleary. Suzy owns Clearwater Farm, another plant-based business in Hesperus. When the plastic greenhouse was damaged in a storm, the Taylors offered to try to fix it. The somewhat lopsided struc-ture now stands close to the Taylor home and is filled with grow lights, dehydration screens, and trays of seedlings.

As Blue Horizons grows, the Taylors want to produce sachets, potpourris, and organic soaps for sale. These are ambitious plans, but for Trent and Linda, working fourteen-hour days is a small price to pay for spending their lives in a garden.

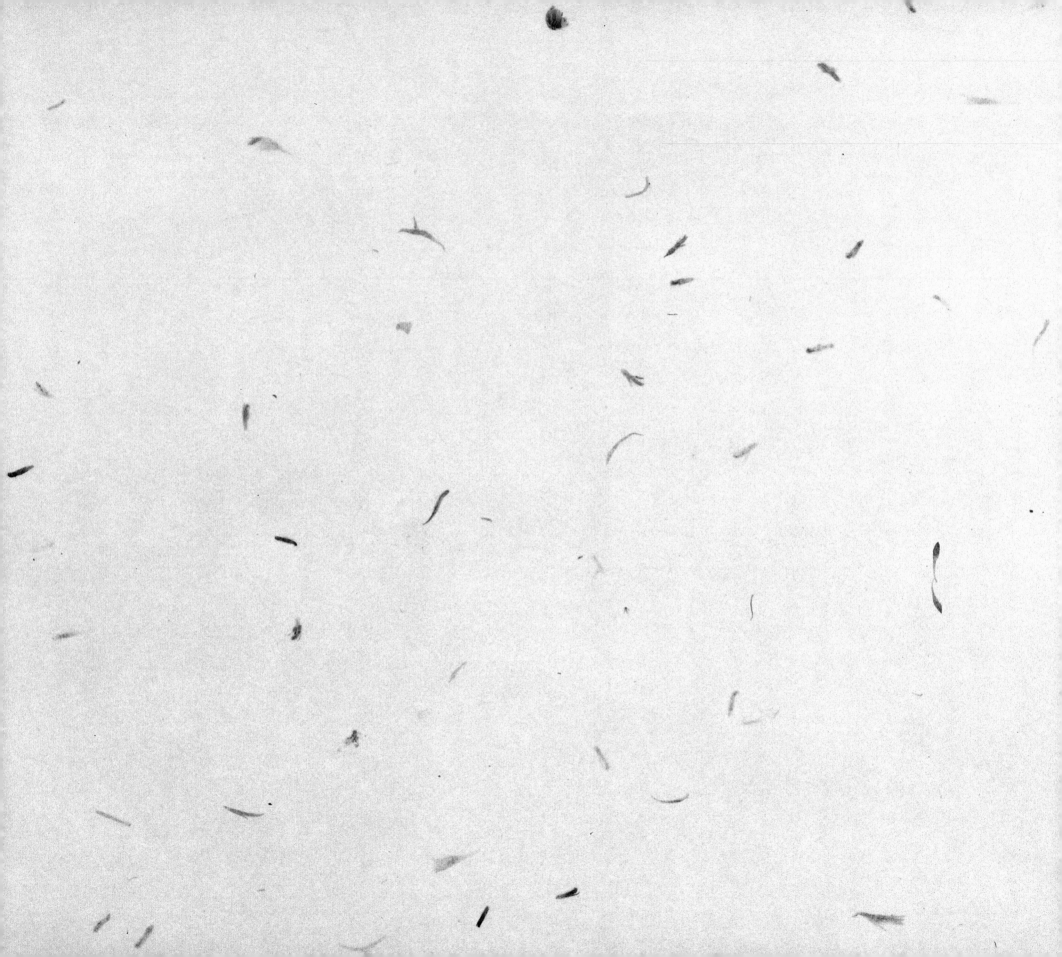